A Grandmother's Essays on Education

Marguerite Morris Willis

iii

The book was printed in the United States of America.

Cover Art: Original quilted wall hanging made by the author for her daughter, the teacher.
Photography by H. H. Paine, Shelburne Falls, MA.
Design layout by sister-in-law Lynn Taylor.
Techno tweeting by nephew Jeff Anderson.
Editorial assistance by Virginia Ray.
Production assistance by Jeff Potter.

To order additional copies of this book, visit Amazon.com

Contents

Dedicated to my late parents
Rosemarie and James Taylor,
my first teachers, who taught me
resourcefulness and creativity.

If knowledge is power, then power is shifting before our very eyes.

Are we unconsciously creating an alien race within our midst?

Schlimmbesserung (a German word that has crossed over into English) - an improvement that makes things worse.

"I never give them (the public) hell. I just tell the truth, and they think it is hell."
— Harry Truman, Look magazine, April 3, 1956

Prologue or Epilogue?

If you have no interest in why I wrote this book, just skip this section and go to Chapter One, as this section also works as an epilogue at the end. It is your choice.

For moments of pure joy, visit an elementary school on the first day of a new school year and watch the littlest ones arrive. Outgoing or shy and everything in between, they all have bright, shining eyes full of light, hope and excitement.

For utter sadness, contrast that with the loss of light in many of those eyes by the end of second grade.

Will another book on education change that?

For some, perhaps. I want to stimulate the debate; however, I do not want to tell anyone how to live. It is my hope that readers will take what they need for their own families. You will see most references are to families. I have done that purposefully. A few years ago a teacher told me about an entire family — grandparents, parents and all the children — attending a parent/teacher conference. This immigrant family from Eastern Europe had a vested

1

interest in the child. The youngest child of the family was the interpreter. That story has been told so many times in the last 150 years but we seem to forget it. Education for our children is a family affair.

In an age when we have professionalized so many occupations or, at minimum, require some sort of licensure, I am suggesting that wise women ways are once again needed.

I have lived through the glory days of JFK, followed by LBJ with the Great Society and the Vietnam War. Less than a decade later in 1972, David Halberstam wrote *The Best and the Brightest* that recounted the hubris of our leaders who thought they knew best. Is it not time to learn to trust ourselves and not depend upon the best and brightest in the political class to tell us how to educate our children?

With the arrogance of a grandmother, this is a challenge to the experts and politicians. With each story, I will raise questions so you may decide what is best for your family. These short narratives of actual practical, personal and public educational experiences have common sense that flows from a life-long interest in education. I have served on

school committees for 15 years and was a volunteer reader in a classroom for seven years in addition to being a mother and grandmother.

Take a quick look on Google to see how many organizations, think tanks and nonprofit institutions are involved in improving education in this country.

It is disconcerting to think about these efforts to improve a system that appears, by evening news reports, to be in disarray in spite all governmental efforts and expenditures. Despair about public education is nothing new. From Horace Mann, the "father of public education," to Tolstoy in Russia, both in the 19th century, we hear similar complaints today.

This book is for a general audience; readers who follow bestseller lists. The collection of short stories is designed to provoke thoughts with which you may agree or disagree. My hope is that it will make you think about your choices for your family's education.

My long, 40-year view serves to depersonalize certain criticisms that need discussion but not direct identification.

I want to initially distinguish individual teachers from any general criticism of education as it exists in this country. As a grandmother, I have observed, personally and professionally, only caring, dedicated people involved in education at the elementary and secondary levels of public education. I can honestly say as individuals that even people with whom I passionately disagree philosophically would be good neighbors. In that, I would also include the many school committee members with whom I have served over the years.

Being a "good neighbor" may be an old-fashioned way of saying they are fine human beings who respect your space but are there if and when you need help. Rural, suburban, urban — wherever you live, even New York City; a collection of small neighborhoods — a neighborhood is our first outside experience in dealing with others.

It is time to stop the political fights over various points in ideology and philosophy. Obtaining majority voter approval does not guarantee a good school program and can, at times, lead to a backlash. We are wasting human and financial resources, time, and energy while producing an inadequate product. The costs do not match the outcomes. All the focus on one system of public education may be part of the problem.

With each new president wanting to put his imprint on education, I think we are seeing a pattern that is actually harmful to education. I find all the political hype to be boring and boorish. Children are in elementary school for such a brief but crucial period of time. They cannot afford these yo-yo movements. Consider the time involved in announcing a new educational initiative, getting the states geared up for it and then implementing it at the local level. That can take three or more years after an inaugural address.

This may sound like an oversimplification but who ever thought one system would fit all?

Even here in rural, western Massachusetts I can drive east 20 miles to find two chain supermarkets, one huge box store, one organic food store and, finally, a completely stocked family-owned small supermarket. Something as simple as food shopping has a range of available options.

4

We can and must have a commitment to public education, but that is not the same as a commitment to one system, bricks and mortar, organizations or jurisdictions.

I have come to see grandmothers as similar to great chefs who welcome the fun of fusion cooking. As such we can look across races, cultures, ethnicity and income and education levels to find commonalities. That is important to me as I see diversity and multicultural movements becoming more divisive than intended. Grandmothers (and grandfathers) want their grandchildren to be successful, however they may define that. The larger culture, and I use that word loosely, is not preparing our children for the future.

Perhaps it is time for grandparents to speak up as we older people, having lived through more than one timeframe, can discern patterns.

As you read the following short chapters, I hope you will think critically about issues raised. Where I have chosen to write personally and within a large timeframe, I would suggest that any reader can substitute his or her story and timeframe on any of the issues raised. Families are their children's first teachers, but that role is not given up at the schoolhouse door the first day of kindergarten or preschool.

When I was very, young, there was a political saying: "the personal is political." Now I feel that the political is personal, and I do not like it. I do not believe in centralized command societies and all that implies for the economy and, particularly, education.

Lest something get lost in translation, I think we can and must have a commitment to an educated populace for this democratic republic's survival — but not necessarily to one system. In the business world, I learned the concept of benchmarking yourself to your most successful competitor. What do others do that you might adopt, adapt or align to your own thinking or operation? We are now competing with the rest of the world for jobs, so it is logical to look at other systems.

We actually need more discussion; not necessarily from the same, usual sources, but from a larger, more varied cross-section. I have lived long enough to know that the mainstream fluctuates, particularly over generations.

Think about this: J.D. Robb, a pseudonym for Nora Roberts, is writing detective mysteries set in the future starting in 2050. There they have droids to perform mundane household tasks. Why do I mention this?

A superintendent (one of many I have know) once postulated to me that in the future we will implant chips in the brains of some human beings so that that they can perform certain tasks. Before anyone has somewhat of a knee-jerk reaction to this, my purpose is to stretch our thinking. The Boomer Generation, if they think about it now, may wonder if "The Jetsons," the TV cartoon show had an early version Skype.

The beauty of science fiction is that you can really do out-of-the-box thinking but it is generally based on a germ of an idea that becomes reality. "Chip Makers Target Everything but the Kitchen Sink" was a headline in the *Wall Street Journal* on January 6, 2011. Today smart phones or universal remotes can control home devices, so how far off is a brain chip? Would you have believed 30 years ago that you could talk to a machine and it would type your words?

So, the question for parents and then indirectly all of us is do you want your child to be a droid or have skills such that they can support themselves and a family? Please note I did not say, "have a meaningful and thoughtful life." The national average for college graduation is about 25 percent depending upon how and where you measure. Then there is seven percent, plus or minus, receiving advanced degrees. I am thinking of the larger, remaining group that will need jobs as well as currently un- or under-employed college graduates. There is a vast difference between having a job and pursuing a career. That is part of the inherent conflict that is not discussed publicly.

The second reason for my writing a book about this is that my voice can get an attitude or tone when I am passionately speaking aloud and that tends to be off-putting to listeners. In writing, I hope that I can be more effective and state the case in a more straightforward manner.

I grew up as a Baby Boomer benefiting from the American inter-generational compact. I would like my grandchildren to receive the same with some tweaking, dusting off old ideas, better use of technology and rounding out with some radically new ideas. I believe that there are many other grandparents who want the same and they must speak up. While I can express many emotions, experiences and editorials, I am not saying that there is only one answer. I am suggesting it is time for more choices so families can find what suits their needs. Ultimately, that is good for our nation.

Daniel Webster, a well-known American statesman and self-described farmer, had his home and law office in Marshfield, MA, where I had the good fortune to reside for 21 years. His words have influenced me for most of adult life: "It is wise to recur to the history of our ancestors. Those who do not look upon themselves as a link connecting the Past with the Future do not perform their duty to the world."

My final reason for writing this book is that several years ago I realized that unresolved discussions with two of my sisters actually reflected what I was seeing in the larger society.

Since the 1970s, my two sisters and I have discussed and debated education in general ultimate agreement. Then in the 1980s on a local cable TV show, I questioned the relatively new concept known as special education because I wondered if we were creating two different classes of students. My daughter, an undergraduate education major, refused to talk to me for days. Thus began a long journey with many disagreements among family members.

That was, until 2009, when I realized my sisters and I had seemingly fallen into the same mindset as our country; pro or con any issue. Each of us had valid points, perspectives, personal and public.

Could we all be correct?

With our current right/left, red/blue, liberal/conservative group thinking, each camp is convinced that its side is in possession of the truth. We have overlooked the possibility that the solution may be in families making their own choices.

Therein lies our political problem with education. It will not be one solution. We need choices so families can meet their personal goals and our country can compete better in the world market with an educated populace.

These are my words based on my experiences, observations and opinions. Where I use others' words, I so note; however, the answers to the questions and choices are the reader's.

"The elementary school must assume as its sublime and most solemn responsibility the task of teaching every child in it to read. Any school that does not accomplish this has failed."
— *William J. Bennett, U.S. Secretary of Education, 1985*

Chapter One

Read to Me, Mom-Mom

"Read to me, Mom-mom," said my five-year-old granddaughter Tess.

"Okay," I said. "Pick out a book." Then I mentally sighed, "Oh, no; not *The Mouse in the House* (Henrietta, A real-life game of hide and seek; copyright 1991, Dorling-Kindersley) again! I had probably read that book to Tess several hundred times, to her older sister Lydia, closer to a thousand — or so it seemed.

With my game face on, we snuggled on the sofa, the big book shared between our laps.

I am not a certified teacher, just a life-long learner. So what is it with this book? Is it the drawings? Is it the mouse tracks inked across the pages? Is it all the rhyming words?

No one explained to me how interactive language is when I was a young mother but I observed my children's abilities to learn. Prior to that, as the oldest of ten children I did play "teacher" at times.

Don't laugh, but I learned to read with Dick and Jane. The key here is to remember that I did learn to read. When I was in fourth grade, my school was saying goodbye to Dick and Jane. The books were offered free for the taking. I was lucky to cart home the extra-large teacher's copy, probably 3x3' in size. It was mounted on a stand so all in the class could see the large print.

I remember my sister Rosemarie telling me once that she remembered me teaching her and our sister Kate with that book. Both sisters recently retired from education after a collective 77 years as teachers and, ultimately, principals at the elementary and high school levels.

In the early 1970s, I learned about a new children's TV show from my cousin Susan. It was called "Sesame Street." This program showed me how ready and able young children were to learn as I watched my own children being drawn into the program. It had an uncanny way of involving viewers, both mothers and children, such that it became an interactive activity. Later I was to learn the difference between passive and interactive TV watching and listening.

From that experience and then a lifetime of more casual and causal learning, I came to see little children's brains like those small, flat, dried pieces of sponge that used to come in the mail promoting this or that product. The sponges (children), when exposed to water (language and ideas), simply blossom, swelling with unknown abilities.

Where there is a particular citation for my writing, I shall give it. However, how do I reference a lifetime of reading? You will see throughout this book that I am a strong admirer of general circulation magazines including *Time, Newsweek,* and *U.S. News* and *Report World* and others.

When my first grandchild was born, I once again had a renewed interest in early childhood learning and found the following articles helpful:

- *U.S. News and World Report* – 6/15/98 – "Baby Talk"
- *Newsweek* -10/27/97 – "Kids Who Can't Learn"
- *Newsweek* – 11/2/98 – "Tomorrow's Child"
- *Newsweek* – 9/7/98 – "Do Parents Matter?"

This is an important fact because I can demonstrate the plethora of information about and on children that has been in the public eye for a very long time. It was this type of reading that initially interested me in young children's abilities to learn. This is not an esoteric matter discussed only in higher education forums or pediatric medicine journals. Now with the Internet and "apps," any adult can do his or her own research.

When reading to preschoolers the first time my ear hears the second rhyming word, I stop and ask the child if that sounds like another word we have just read. Trust me; the little ones very quickly get the idea of rhyming.

With my first grandchild, when we were driving anywhere when she was little, we would do rhyming games. It starts so simply with *at, bat, cat* and before you know it, the child comes up with *fat, mat* or *sat.*

It started as a game. We talked about words that sounded alike. I told my granddaughter that this is called rhyming. You can work up to more letters and longer words. This is also the start of building vocabulary but more importantly, overall verbal skills. This is something a pre-school or kindergarten teacher will notice right away; actually, assessments are made by the schools. So the first question for families is "what is done with those assessments"? How do those assessments drive classroom activities? What is done for the individual child with poor verbal skills? Conversely, what is done for the highly verbal child? "We do the best we can for every child" is not a satisfactory response to an education question.

If no one is actually talking with and to a child, it is very difficult to develop language skills. In some cases, the language that develops is very inappropriate. Besides listening, children are always watching us.

I live in a very rural area with a lot of dirt roads winding around and over mountains. I am not sure that city people will understand this but here we appreciate our natural beauty. It is routine to get in your truck and take a drive once in a while to check out the scenery. Sometimes we look for moose, wild turkeys or other wildlife; or, we might be checking out the changing foliage or ice encrusted trees and hills while listening to the radio or CD player. My musical tastes cover a broad range of types from Alternative to Zydeco. I particularly enjoy Vivaldi's

"Four Seasons." Truth be told, I like to conduct. I tell you this because one day I looked over to see my two-year-old granddaughter also conducting with her little arms moving in time with the music.

Language starts in infancy with sounds, syntax and semantics actually imprinted on babies' brains before they ever utter a word. This continues and is most intensive in the first three years. It is not what a child may hear, but rather what is said to the baby. That is a clear distinction. It cannot be as passive as is TV. It must be interactive, engaging the child. TV can be interactive for the child if an adult is talking with the child as to what they are seeing or hearing. Can some "talk" to a child be gibberish? Of course! Think of a grandmother cooing soft sounds to an infant. Singsong nursery rhymes are another prerogative of a grandmother and may actually be more productive than special TV shows or videos for baby because the grandmother is interacting with the child.

But when they develop their first favorite books that they frequently seek out, I am grateful and know I have done my work well. Also I have found with the little ones the so-called board books are a great way to give them a book to hold without any concern for torn pages. And that is the start of making a small child a willing, engaged and happy reader.

Before any child ever enters a school so much of that child's future successes will be determined to a great degree by what happens in the early childhood years from birth to three years. No school official can or will ever say that publicly. They will tell you that they take each child as given to them and then they work for the child's fullest potential. Yes, that is true, but missing from our national discussion is just how much occurs before they even enter school. In the child's first year of life about 50 percent of the brain develops. While there are many factors affecting that period of brain development, such as diet and exercise, an important source of brain stimulation is someone reading to the child.

The next major growth of brain cells is in the next two years. So whenever a child enters a school system, be it at age 3, 4, 5 or 6, the most crucial learning years for brain growth have already occurred — before the age of three. So there it is: assuming no disability, a child's brain can be stimulated or not in the first three years of life and once in school, he or she may make progress, but the starting points can and will be vastly different.

I am not talking about creating baby geniuses. I am writing about the ability of a child to learn to listen to a story being read aloud, how to roll a ball, how to hop on one foot, how to speak in sentences – nothing complicated. But when it is not done, it holds back brain growth.

I am suggesting that we have this discussion soon as I am hearing calls from the federal Health and Human Services Secretary Kathleen Sebelius for universal preschool. While preschool is the norm is some states, it is not the answer for children in need. It is the wrong solution for the wrongly diagnosed problem. The problem in the majority of situations is within the first three years.

If the problem is daycare, then let us have a discussion about that, but do not wrap it into a warm and fuzzy educational blanket. Unless you want a state run nursery, families might discuss how to address these early crucial years of care.

I probably could not have written those words five years ago, but our world is changing. How many families are multi-generational now for economic reasons? I guess we can say this is the economical issue of early childhood care. Families will do what needs to be done to care for one another.

During the major time for brain development from birth to three, a doctor, one hopes, will be checking for certain mileposts, such as when and if crawling starts. But the point is, who, what and how it is done or not done can be debated until the cows come home. There is a need within our society to have this discussion. Fifty-plus years ago in a civics class we were taught that the family is the basic unit of a society; perhaps grandparents can help their families figure out solutions for more stimulation for the young children.

Many years ago I made a proposal to a principal that we use a form letter with birth congratulations along with a two-page summary about how to start preparing the child for school. I wondered if the PTO could pay for a yearlong subscription to a parenting-type magazine, as I had been paying for one at our local library.

But what if we informed new parents in the hospital nursery, or by letter, or some other way, that the local school may reasonably expect, barring any disability, their child by age four to:

1. Know her full name.
2. Know her full address.
3. Be able to hop on one foot.
4. Be able to roll a ball to another.
5. Know the front of a book from the back.

These points are not original to me. They are five that I remember from a list of ten that I saw years ago. It was an article in a newspaper in Alaska in August 1999. I had traveled there with my brother Steve and his family. It was a front-page article and caught my eye. Alaska was just instituting a statewide kindergarten program. The newspaper interviewed one of the teachers and asked her how she would assess the children's readiness and needs. The teacher devised her own little ten-step interview. I was struck by the simplicity of it while also seeing how informative it would be. Over time I have forgotten half of the points but sometimes it seems to me that I can over assess. It was the simplicity of her test that is the message that needs to be out there.

Is it time to let parents know what is expected and, if the child, barring any disability, cannot do these five things, should their permanent record so indicate? This should be part of any accountability process for schools and teachers. Also parents should be informed that the school's responsibility will be only to show annual progress. With calls for merit pay, I firmly believe there must be an accounting of how the child arrives at any school initially.

Why would I even suggest this? Some will deem it extreme, however it is needed to be in the general discussion as it can and does affect us all. For example, if your child knows how to brush his or her teeth, do you want him sitting in a class on tooth brushing in pre-school or kindergarten?

Over the years I have interacted with many young mothers. When I ask if they have been to the library with, for example, a ten-month-old infant, I basically get a glazed-over look more often than not.

Then I generally comment on how smart babies are, what wonderful board books are available at our local library, and say that looking at books will actually help the child later when she goes to school. As I see it, those mothers who "hated school" and who do not like to read themselves because of painful school memories will not see any value in this for their children. For whatever reasons, books and reading are associated with college-bound children.

I read something recently that referred to the early years when children are learning to read that said by fourth grade, they read to learn. How succinct is that? What better reason to make sure that reading is the primary focus at the elementary school level?

Since so many young parents I meet do not like to read, our challenge is to let them know that their children must learn to read to be able to work. The challenge is to find an acceptable means of communicating this idea.

Early in my regional school committee tenure we had a report from the physical education teachers from all the elementary schools that feed into the middle/high school complex. Of great note to me was a mention that 50 percent of kindergarten children needed remedial gym classes. Not being a wallflower, I asked what that meant. We were told that half of the kindergarten children did not know how to roll a ball.

Are our schools directly responsible for the 50% who needed remedial physical education in kindergarten? Of course not, but we do have to provide services to address the deficiency. This is one very small example of schools attempting to adjust for what was or was not done at home. This has long-term consequences and costs for the child and the school. At what point is it time for us to talk about this?

For me, it is discouraging in private conversations with educators to hear them always come back to the argument, "We must do this for them regardless of whomever is responsible or else the children suffer." Or they will say, "If we don't do this, who will?" In that vein of goodness is the inherent snag that enables the problems to become statistically worse for the children.

One of my favorite (of many) memories as a grandmother is sitting on the living room carpet with my 15-month-old granddaughter and teaching her how to roll a ball. So much of what is not being done with children is not rocket science. It is these simple actions that help the child to develop eye and hand coordination. Have we as a society forgotten that infants and children need some simple attention?

I have noticed that swaddling has made a comeback. For me, it reflects an ancient understanding that infants need to be held.

Is it interference in parental rights to let them know that we expect the child to arrive at school knowing their names, addresses and telephone numbers? Is it too much to expect that a child can roll a ball?

Beyond the hyperbole in the musical "The Music Man," there is trouble in River City. The signs are everywhere, yet politicians suggest that we spend more on education. I contend that we have not correctly identified problems, such as lack of ball rolling. Is there any surprise that we come up with wrong solutions?

Referring back to my earlier droid example, similar to R2D2 in "Star Wars," not Verizon's newest cell phone, is it somehow possible for schools to explain to parents that their child may become a droid later in life if certain things are not done within the first three years? I know lawyers will never allow that but I am free to raise the issue. It may strike some as extreme or harsh, but a conversation needs to occur. The "how" of it I leave to others; perhaps religious groups could encourage congregants to work with small children in their neighborhoods or towns.

The problems are only getting worse. I understand the tension between individual and family rights and schools' responsibilities to show progress as determined by achievement scores. This is not about whose child will go to college. It is about every child having success in the learning process. As a school committee member, parents have informed me that their child is not going to college and they do not need to do a lot of schoolwork. Whatever work people pursue, they will need to know how to read at a minimum level, yet parents who hated school generally will not and do not see any value in education.

With one young mother, I took the initiative and bought a big picture book for her ten-month-old infant. Several weeks later she told me how much the little one loved the book, particularly the animal pictures.

That is a perception problem and part of our problem in public education. I think back to my Mother, who made distinctions as to types of learners. She was aware and respectful of hands-on learning and street smarts. While educators speak of multiple kinds of intelligence and are expected to incorporate differentiated teaching methods, it is my observation that is not done in everyday practice.

I do know of one teacher, though, who had a child arrive in her fourth-grade class with a record of limited abilities. I do not recall all the specifics but she did learn that the child had a very special relationship with a grandfather who was also a farmer. With that knowledge, the teacher used a seed catalogue to help the child with his reading. He enthusiastically took to the task then because it had meaning for him.

Referring back to my droid example, how will we as a society find the balance in having someone responsible for the first three years of life? I am seriously looking for effective but respectful ways to stop wasting our little sponges. There is an inherent risk to identifying the problem. Bill Cosby suffered slings and arrows when he suggested that parents need to parent. But if it is not being done at home, how much do we want the schools involved — or worse, held responsible?

If you read 10-15 minutes to a very young child on a regular basis, by the age of three, the child will know the front of a book from the back. If you hand that child a book upside down and backwards, he will automatically turn it to the correct position. I call this visual knowledge. Children recognize how letters should look without even knowing their letters.

I was discussing this with another grandmother who also served many, many years on a school committee. She insisted that her grandchildren could do that at age two! No need to debate the age; I'm sure you take my point. A child can acquire that skill if he or she is exposed to books, e-books or iPhone kids' apps being read to them.

I can see some young mothers rolling their eyes and thinking, "Oh boy, another thing to add to my day." I do understand how busy and different home life is these days but we are talking about the child's future. Is that worth 15 minutes of your time?

If you think of reading too structurally, you will miss everyday opportunities. I was reminded of this the other day. I looked at *People* magazine while in a doctor's waiting room recently that showed all the designer dresses for the Academy Awards. It struck me as a perfect opportunity to point out colors to a child.

Without this investment by parents, family members or friends, the child will be behind from the very first day of school. If you do not personally know a teacher, visit a school and ask the principal about this. We all — parents, taxpayers, local officials and teachers — have a vested interest in getting this right.

Additionally, reading aloud to a child also prepares the little one for the classroom because the child is learning also how to sit still. With technology so pervasive today, we are seeing a generation that is used to being constantly stimulated. Clearly I am not talking about sitting at desks all day. Classrooms are set up very differently now in ways that allow for a lot of movement. But I am seeing many, and sometimes a majority, of students who cannot sit still for ten minutes. Again, ask a teacher about this and the difficulties it causes with overall classroom management.

Recently, Secretary Kathleen Sebelius called our national attention to that fact that we have too many five-year-olds who cannot sit still for ten minutes. Hence, she said, we need universal pre-school for three and four year olds. I disagree strongly with her conclusions. The "learning to sit still" starts much earlier than pre-school. For those who like to do their own research, check out arguments made 20 and 30 years ago for kindergarten. I suggest that you may find similar arguments now being used for pre-school.

For me, this is a solution that does not address the problem. This leads to a waste of time, resources and money. A child learns to sit still when he is read to or shown books by family members in the first three years.

For many years, I was a volunteer reader to a second-grade class and that will be a reference point in several places in this book. For the purposes of this chapter, I say unequivocally that, assuming no severe learning disabilities, a child's educational experience will depend upon the homework done in the first three years.

I support the concept of merit pay for teachers, however, I would personally insist on establishing a child's baseline data to measure how prepared the child was when she first entered school. My discourse may go from theoretical to everyday talk, but I think we need a blend of practical versus theory in this broad discussion of education.

When a child with limited verbal skills first comes to school, we know that the child has encountered little language. Language is not acquired just by watching TV. It requires speaking with others.

Think about a public service ad currently running on TV showing a young father shopping with a little one in the cart's seat. He is naming items as he places them in the cart. In the dairy section he picks up cheese, turns to the child, and says, "Can you say gorgonzola?" with a big smile. The child, about age two, giggles and says something like "go-gan-zol-a." The father has made a game that he plays with the child while shopping. He is talking **with** the child. And that is one example of how a child learns language even before talking. All children need to know of our language is essentially being imprinted that first year.

Recently, I read to my grandson Sam. He had received this wonderful book from my sister Kate as a Christmas present. It is an interesting concept based on life-sized animals. How does one get life-sized animals in a book? It starts with small animals, but quickly, as sizes increase, the focus is only on a certain part of an animal.

It was fascinating to see the actual pores on the skin of a rhinoceros' face around his horn. Together we learned that the horn is really only a hairy bundle and not a bone. On each side of the double-sided pages there was a lot of information, including Latin names. This was an opportunity in two ways: I could show Sam how to break up a word into syllables so he could sound out any word and I could talk about an old language not spoken anymore but used by scientists to name plants and animals.

This made perfect sense to my seven-year-old grandson. He did most of the reading of the facts, so we had a learning and sharing experience but what he learned will surely bubble up at a later time, such as, "Latin is an old language not spoken anymore but used by scientists." I am so certain of this because my 15-year-old granddaughter had a similar experience recently. On a biology quiz, she remembered facts from a series on animals that I had read to her when she was about seven. That is such a joyous experience for a grandparent.

This process of talking about what we see is also a way to increase a child's vocabulary. It can be talking about tools, cars, carpentry work, engineering, fishing, hunting, sewing, golfing and the weather. WHATEVER! Caps for emphasis; I'm not yelling. Language will be acquired before the child ever speaks. Reading will help, but so will plain, old-fashioned talking. And families can do this if they are made aware of the need and the results.

A preschooler sees an animal book as a fun experience. That sense of enjoyment can carry over so the child sees reading as pleasurable. This attitude prepares them for school and more learning.

There was an ad a long time ago for financial services that said it measured success one client at a time. And so it can be with each and every child if he or she hears short, nighttime stories. That will be an important start for that child's future successes.

I can still see in my mind's eye my daughter at age four going into the children's library by herself to return her book while I went to the adult library to return mine. Our car was parked between the two library buildings.

Somewhat typical of so many old New England towns, the library started in 1895 with a legacy from a citizen for a library and other public uses. The library moved in 1940 to an old school building on a main thoroughfare. Much later a small home next door became a children's library.

My daughter had been using the library for about a year. The children's library cards were kept on file at the front desk. Returning books involved putting your books on a small table next to the front desk. After a child picked out his selections, he gave his name to the desk attendant who checked out the books.

This particular day I suggested that my daughter go in by herself. I believed in challenging children. She initially struggled with the idea. I assured her that her father would wait in the car while I went into the big library. I returned to the car before her. Within minutes she came skipping out, her face positively beaming with excitement. She climbed into the back seat. We asked how it went. Her reply sums up a child's joy with her own accomplishment. "I felt like a five year old," my four-year-old daughter replied.

That is my family's story. What will yours be? In our changing demographics, will we see devotional Hinduism and its storytelling used by some families? Or, at Passover, will Jews tell the Exodus story to their children? Storytelling is as old as mankind, yet we seemingly are forfeiting our right to tell our stories to our younger family members. What stories do you want your family's children to hear, know, understand and, ultimately, appreciate? Or will you use old movies, such as "Moses" and "The Ten Commandments?" Or will your family read Harry Potter? JK Rowling borrowed from so many cultures. That may appeal to you. Ask yourself why children so flocked to that series. It is a wonderfully woven story of good and evil that children recognized, respected and related to current events. Children have an inherent need to understand the world where they live, the people in it and relationships among people.

Do any of the words In Disney's "The Lion King" resonant with you? I particularly appreciate Mufasa's words to Zimba, "Remember who you are," as a way to transmit your own belief in a family member's potential.

I write this not to advocate for any particular viewpoint, but to highlight that parents need to know who they are in their own beliefs and reinforce them in their own homes. I started casual discussions with my first granddaughter before she ever went to school by subtly emphasizing this is what our family values . . .appreciates . . .believes in . . .expects from her — all in an effort to create those distinctions. Another way to express this is how my Mother did. She said to me hundreds of time when we were young, "If everyone jumped off a bridge, would you?"

What will you read to your family's children to inspire them? Or are you going to let others decide what and how to inspire or entertain them?

I love reading mysteries for simple pleasure and relaxation. When I started to read to the second-graders, I used myself as a model. I thought, "If I like mysteries, I wonder if they would?" I found several series of age-appropriate mystery books. The *A to Z Mysteries* is a great way to introduce a child to choosing a book for himself. I discussed the cover art with the children and let them know that sometimes the picture catches your attention and makes you think it could be a good story.

Mostly I gave them permission to choose. Required reading is schoolwork. Reading for pleasure is something I like to cultivate with young readers.

When I finished the first in a series, I then showed them an index of all the other stories that they might like. For me the key is "like." I strive to make reading a fun activity for the young ones. When a child tells me on a Monday morning that he went to the library over the weekend to get another book in a series, my work is done.

How does your family feel about reading? Do you think reading is only with books? Do you like sports magazines? What about home decorating magazines? Think about what you like and consider sharing with your children. What do you want them to read? How will your family help your children to learn to read so that they will be able to learn all their lives? What choices, small or large, will your family make to help your children before they go to school?

"I talk and talk and talk, and I haven't taught people in 50 years what my father taught by example in one week."
— Mario Cuomo, Governor of New York, Time,
June 2, 1986

"Wonder is the desire for knowledge."
— Thomas Aquinas (1255-1274)

Chapter Two
Geography – Where in the World?

Sometime around 1986 my daughter came home from college all excited. She had this great class and a fascinating teacher. It was a subject she never had previously in school herself but she loved this class. In my mind's eye, I can still see the excitement on her face and I was curious.

"What is the subject?" I asked.

"Geography," she replied.

Then I realized she was right in finding this subject new and exciting. Geography had become passé. It was one of my favorite subjects when I was in school. I particularly liked working with maps. Maybe that is why I am able to navigate anywhere without electronic assistance and why I have an understanding of the evening news about other remote places in the world.

I have been thinking about this. There are many reasons so many younger people are not involved as citizens. Perhaps not knowing much about other countries, including their locations, does not help.

In addition to my own 40-year interest and perspective on education, I have chosen the long time frame to de-personalize criticism of the entire educational system. But the point here is that someone, somewhere, in the halls of education decided that geography was no longer important in the late 1970s into the early 1980s. Thus the teaching of geography disappeared for Generation X (born 1965-1980). As no one was ever responsible for that decision, my second point is that it will also be the case now and in the future when other changes are made. No one is responsible; we simply move onto something we are told is newer, better and improved. All too often this happens without a critique of what did or did not work.

We can all make mistakes, but why is it that so many private schools still focus on a classical education? If you really want to get frustrated, try the math debates of the last 30 years. We are talking about trends. After a certain age, we all have seen trends come and go with basically little to no accountability. Caught in this, though, are children, such as my daughter who did not have geography until college when she chose it herself.

For our children to compete in this world, they first must know something of its geography. Perhaps as a start it would be helpful if they knew the geography of their own states. I have heard from my daughter, the teacher, that frequently students do not know the geography of their hometowns.

It is not difficult to include geography for even little ones. When reading stories from around the world to my second graders, I used a pull-down, wall world map or a globe. Second graders still are enthusiastic learners, so a quick show and tell with the map or globe satisfies their natural curiosity and gives them a larger perspective. Children are capable of so much. I generally started with an outline of Massachusetts, then moved on to the United States of America and finally, to North America. So I introduced the concept of state, country and continent.

They quickly grasped the idea. I then could say "today's story is from China and that is in Asia." Since I already explained that each country is in a different color, I could give a hint about the color of China. Or I said, "it is the largest country in Asia." That enabled the student to find China. All of this can be done conversationally and with a sense of curiosity, as I was not the teacher, just a friend who came into the classroom to read for 15-20 minutes. Twenty minutes would be the maximum; although, on some days I asked if they had wiggle worms for lunch because what else could explain all the squiggling? Humor aside, though, it is challenging. Sometimes the well-behaved child can feel annoyance at all the disruptions, particularly if someone is reading a story that has captured the imagination.

A real public service is now being offered by network and cable news shows when maps are included in those news presentations. It is effective to have a country initially highlighted on a world map, then zoom in for a closer look, with neighboring countries identified. This idea of using and showing maps is not new. President Franklin D. Roosevelt made a radio speech that became known as "the map speech." He asked his fellow

Americans listening to him to have a map in front of them as he talked about the location of battle lines.

For our children to **compete** in this world, they first must know something of its geography. Yes, I have used the word compete. Someone's feelings may be hurt in that process but it is the way of human beings. Kumbaya moments do not fit into this discussion. As a child in the 1950s, I was told to eat all the food on my plate because children were hungry in China. To give this a current context, my sister Rosemarie, at one of her school committee meetings, used as her last slide in a power-point presentation this sentence: "Study hard because there is a child in India or China who wants your job."

Now, with the advent of GPS in cars, most people no longer use maps. As you might suspect, I do. Since I travel back and forth to New Jersey from Massachusetts, I sometimes seek an alternate route if there is a traffic jam. Once, to the annoyance of my granddaughter and a niece, I asked them to help me find another route in my U.S. atlas. I talked them through it, starting with finding the page for Connecticut and other pertinent points, such as the mileage scale so they could gauge that. I also mentioned that we wanted to go north. Yes, they grumbled, but what will they do when there is a technology blackout? For instance, watch when power goes out in a retail store and cashiers do not know how to make change between the sale price and money tendered.

I think map reading is still an important skill and, as part of a geography lesson, can spark the imagination of a child and prepare for citizenship.

Generation Y (born 1981-1999) after Generation X seems to have a little more interest in geography because of such software as Google Earth, Facebook Friends around the world, and satellite TV directly from other countries, such as Al Jazeera TV. I wonder what popped into people's minds when they heard or saw the February 2011 political events in Egypt with the demand for Mubarack to step down as president. Cell phones brought that news to the world.

While so many of us in this country have forgotten about geography, world demographics have been changing rapidly and significantly. Will those changes affect us? How do those changes affect our ability to compete in the global marketplace?

Consider that the median age in the United States is 36.8, as opposed to a median age of 24 in Egypt as of 2010. Now think about the faces you saw in the streets protesting. If half of your population is under age 24 with males un- or underemployed, do the pictures/videos make more sense? It has long been theorized that most periods of world unrest occur in societies with a youth bulge that is unemployed.

Details including demographics, employment statistics, climate, terrain, transportation, natural resources, imports and exports are all part of geography.

Good teachers know a teachable moment when it fortuitously happens. Geography has been returned to our state curriculum so that Generation Y is starting to see where they are in the world.

My daughter was teaching geography to her 4th-grade class. In the course of her presentation she covered imports and exports, but felt she did not have their attention. She suggested that they take their sneakers off, look inside, and see where the sneaker was made. If memory serves me correctly, she told me later that all the sneakers came from China. That lesson on imports/exports will not fade away. When those children are adults, I contend that they will understand a news report about trade imbalances because at some level they will remember their sneakers.

I live in rural, western Massachusetts — the Wild West frontier territory in the colonial days of our American history. Our American colonial history becomes real in a child's mind as local features, such as mountains, valleys and rivers, were a vital part of that history. For example, the Connecticut River was the major means of transportation from the Atlantic coast through Connecticut, into Massachusetts, north into Greenfield and Northfield, and then becoming the boundary between Vermont and New Hampshire —before any roads were built. River trade included 18th-century, custom-made, Connecticut Valley furniture, including high chests, side chairs and secretaries with claw-and-ball feet and cabriole legs.

Trade such as that provided jobs for many people. This is not an esoteric or trivial piece of information. Where will our children work? What kind of work will be available? It seems to me that we may have something in common today with the Egyptians in that they also have many highly educated young people with no work. It also seems that we have separated work and education — or will we have a Diaspora such as that which dispersed the Irish around the world until they could come home again to jobs created by the low corporate tax rate in the 1980s? Also, with TV shows such as "House Hunters International" on the airwaves, retirees and children can see what is available elsewhere at what price.

But the point of this chapter is more than just discussing the subject of geography. It is to offer the concrete example of a decision made by a group (probably) that has directly impacted the education of a generation and to point out the many ways in which we live now with the consequences.

How will your family monitor or accept these types of group decisions that may or may not reflect what you think is an important educational component?

In my religious upbringing in the Catholic Church, we learned about the concept of the "devil's advocate." In essence, it is the person charged with developing an opposing viewpoint to the larger perspective. I see a role for those who question new programs. All too often, if and when you question, you may be criticized as "anti-education." Still, I believe that our school systems need to be challenged and held accountable. It is crucial that all new programs be evaluated before we lose a generation of kids based on mistaken concept, premise, or someone's idea of a "new" program.

How will you be a devil's advocate for your family's education? How does your local public school curriculum match with that of the nearest private school? How many new math programs has your local school used in the last twenty years? Has your school ever told you as a parent that they don't expect you to understand what is being taught in math class? Are you satisfied with the answers you are given?

Why is it important to ask questions?

My daughter's generation in Massachusetts' high schools also had smoking courts outside their classrooms. What were we thinking? Actually, we were also talking about "global cooling" in those days.

I mention this not to be contentious, but to ask you to contemplate changes in thinking in your own lifetimes. The higher you estimate your own personal life odometer reading may well correlate with how many cycles you've seen.

"Let me be a free man. Free to travel. Free to stop. Free to work. Free to choose my own teachers. Free to follow the religion of my fathers. Free to think and talk and act for myself – and I will obey every law or submit to the penalty."
— Chief Joseph, Nez Perce 1840-1904

"And for the support of this declaration, with a firm reliance on the protection of divine providence, we mutually pledge to each other our lives, our fortunes, and our sacred honor."
— *Thomas Jefferson in the Declaration of Independence, July 4, 1776*

"It were not best that we should all think alike; it is difference of opinion that makes horse races."
— *Mark Twain, "Pudd'nhead Wilson," 1894*

Chapter Three

Bible Studies or Western Civilization?

More than a year before the February 2011 political uprisings in northern Africa and the Middle East I had started a file of notes and ideas for chapters of this book even though I was working on another book.

An actual family situation prompted my notes for this chapter.

My granddaughter was frustrated with her freshman history class that dealt with more current events than history in the Middle East. She could not keep the cast of characters, organizations or countries straight in her mind. Then I realized that she had no solid knowledge of the Old Testament of the Bible. My reference to the Old Testament is a clue to my background. How could anyone comprehend the politics of that part of the world without knowing something about Abraham, Moses, the Persians, Israelites, Philistines, Egyptians, Babylonians, Turks and others?

In my parochial grade school in Philadelphia in the 1950s, we read stories from the Old Testament of the Bible. It was part of a religion class, but it did double duty with reading aloud, although I now see it also as an ancient history class. I can still see in my mind the drawings of the ancient gardens at Babylon. My imagination was sparked as we learned about Mesopotamia, the ancient Persian people, their culture and the whole picture of the beginnings of our so-called Western Civilization.

In the 1960s and 1970s, we started to hear mantras that dead white men's history was not important anymore.

While I am writing about a part of humanity's religious stories, I do not want to preclude the human element within all religions. In *"God Is Not One – The Eight Rival Religions That Run the World – and Why Their Differences Matter"* by Stephen Prothero, he notes that "[many] see calling order out of chaos as a political task [to be done] by secular means . . . but for most of human history [including Confucianism and Vedic religions], "ritual is the glue that holds society together." I am not excluding anyone. I am writing that with which I have some familiarity.

Sometimes I feel as if I am repeatedly filling in the blanks of spotty knowledge for my children and grandchildren. It is the ignorance level that disturbs me. I know as a life-long learner that the generations following us are not as literate as we were, nor do they possess as much basic knowledge about our humanity and how that plays out in various civilizations.

I am not alone in this thinking. David McCullough, a writer who makes history read like a novel, contends that our young people are, by and large, historically illiterate.

I admit that the current younger generations are quicker with technology, — so much so that many early game players have become today's advanced micro-surgeons — but technology does not explain their humanity.

The focus of this chapter is historical knowledge transmitted through the generations.

Each new generation, it seems, is always surprised by economic turmoil, yet in Genesis we read, "there shall arise seven years of famine." This is not a promotion for religious teaching, but it is important that mankind's stories be told — whatever the sources, as our stories have always helped us to understand ourselves.

If the cradle of Western civilization was ancient Mesopotamia, currently the Middle East, perhaps an understanding of the first would make the second more understandable. Why? Why do I use the word "understandable?" Perhaps because today's voters may need to have some understanding when they listen to presidential candidates debate foreign affairs before an election. In 1985 President Jimmy Carter wrote in *The Blood of Abraham – Insights into the Middle East* about the common bond of three major religions. That is, for me, a perfect example of making history, even ancient history, relevant for students. Otherwise, how will our children know the history of the Middle East?

Theoretically, one reason for public education is to have an educated populace to maintain our democratic republic. I do wonder, though, when TV reporters and even politicians refer to this country as a democracy what the impact of those words is on our children's and grandchildren's understanding of this country?

When they speak incorrectly, I often think of Ben Franklin's purported response to a woman on Chestnut Street, in Philadelphia, outside the Constitutional Convention who asked him, "What did the convention create?" Franklin is reported to have said, "A republic, Madam, if you can keep it." Yet if one surveyed U.S. students, I daresay most would say we live in a democracy. Words matter. We are a democratic republic.

Another annoyingly ignorant comment generally heard after national elections is that the total vote for President should prevail. That statement alone should make us wonder what is being taught to our children. Every time someone in my presence refers to our "democracy," I remind him that we are a democratic republic. Just because something is repeated and repeated does not make it so.

Admittedly I am old school, but "anything goes" or "whatever" does not fly anymore. I see that as destructive to our society.

One summer I took a young granddaughter to see some American history. I was very disappointed with part of the tour guide's talk in the House of Burgesses in Colonial Williamsburg. When I was a young student, I was fascinated with the passion of Patrick Henry's speech in the House of Burgesses. The actual building is still available to visit. Perhaps you have been there, but for those who have not, I'll explain.

As each tour group entered the Hall, everyone was asked to take a seat. As the guide began her discourse, we were all asked to stand. Then all women were instructed to sit, followed by tenant framers, and slaves. Who remained standing in the House of Burgesses? Only white men who owned property. Most folks at the presentation I attended appropriately tut-tut-ed and comments were made as to what barbarians we were back then.

This is a prime example of how political correctness is shaping, coloring and distorting history with current perspectives instead of telling the story. For my granddaughter and me, our experience together in living history became an opportunity to share my knowledge and perspective on that time.

The House of Burgesses was an idea based on the English Parliament, so there is no surprise there. But you cannot read the words spoken in that Hall that preceded our American Revolution and not have great admiration — if you realize how new an idea it was then. To compare that time with now is a deliberate distortion.

Soon after, taxation without representation was becoming unacceptable to some, although certainly not all felt that way. It was a new concept. We do our children a disservice by presenting 17th-century history with a 21st-century perspective. However, a discussion of taxation without representation could be turned on its head today with a discussion of contemporary representation without taxation.

In the relative scheme of things time-wise, this country is still an experiment. We are not even 250 years old.

George Washington, in his first inaugural address on April 30, 1789, told us "the preservation of the sacred fire of liberty, and the destiny of the republican model of government, are justly considered as deeply, perhaps, as finally staked, on the experiment entrusted to the hands of the American people."

We are a very young country. United States history, as opposed to that of earlier people living in the Americas, is a brief period in the history of mankind.

To put this in contemporary perspective, in the early 1990s during the Bosnia-Herzegovina-Serbia conflict, all parties could recite their historic grievances — going back to the 9th century. Those various parties included Muslims, Orthodox Christians, Jews and Catholics, Slovenians, Albanians, Rumanians, Croatians, Serbians, Montenegrens, Armenians, Greeks, Bulgarians, Turks, Czechs, and Slovaks. I have also heard the entirety referred to as the Balkans Peninsula. If I have left out any other minor players, it is not intended. The list of names of all the tribes, before the naming of nations, is huge, but artificial country boundaries in the 19th century did not eliminate all groups' tribal memories.

Even after the peace talks' so-called successful conclusion, United Nations peacekeeping troops are still today in Sarajevo. The last number I heard was 16,000 peacekeepers! I seriously wonder if we have learned anything from that event, but I also understand why the average person simply blocks this out. It is simply overwhelming. Of note is that the entire area is divided legally among ethnic groups today, but, even as my great-grandfather, an Englishman, married an Irish-American woman in 1877, I wonder when there will be Romeo and Juliet stories in this part of the world.

I know I was so confused by televised news reports about the Bosnia conflict but an opportunity to know more came for me in the winter of 1993-94.

A reporter who had spent time a lot of time in the Balkans came to speak on a Sunday afternoon at the Arms Library in Shelburne Falls, MA. I listened intently but still could not grasp the "how" of reported ethnic cleansing. Finally, I said, "Pardon my ignorance, but all the people look the same on the news, so please tell me how they did know who to kill when ethnic cleansing occurred in villages?'

The answer stunned me; however, it might have made a current events class sit up and pay attention had students heard the same response. Each group who cleansed (Read: killed) had a copy of the

44

federal Yugoslavian 1990 census in which everyone was required to list ethnic background and religion. No group tolerated "mixed" families. This was not one group reporting on another. It was a government list that provided that information.

Imagine the class discussion about this horrifying news. Do you think we could grab high school students' attention and imaginations if then we used our own government information on race, ethnicity, income, religion and percentages of total? Because various government agencies cull that information on a fairly regular basis here too. Oh, but we are "the good guys." Or is that denying our own humanity? Part of that humanity includes fear. We have embarrassment about the internment of Japanese-Americans during WWII but also quietly buried the facts that west coast Italian Americans were also interned in restricted living areas in the early year of the War. There was talk of expanding those internments of Italians on the east coast, but that ended when an advisor asked FDR, "Do you want to explain to the American people why you interned Joe DiMaggio's mother?"

None of this is esoteric. It is pertinent, here and now, and crucial knowledge that Generations X and Y will need to live in this world as we all continue to deal with age-old battles among human beings.

As an example, there exist Irish families in this country who speak intimately of the 1916 Easter Sunday Irish Uprising as if it were yesterday. That is a perfect example of a collective memory that becomes passed from generation to generation. It is also true of the Jews and Palestinians, but it is not true here in the United States, if you look at high school textbooks.

We are also seeing the re-writing of classics. That seems to be accepted without much challenge. Major publishers acknowledged this when they announced the "N" word was being deleted from Mark Twain's classic *Tom Sawyer*.

These kinds of constraints on language, with re-writing of history, are getting a little scary. Who is defining what is acceptable speech and why? Is it okay to erase a cultural memory because it is distasteful or deemed politically incorrect by some? Will thoughts be next? Have you noticed how people have become so politically correct that they avoid expressing a thought? I have actually heard people refer to some words as being too negative. When will "they," the mysterious "they" who make these proclamations, eliminate the very word "negative?" In my experience, doing this is also a way to shut down any debate by simply labeling a school critic as "too negative."

But let us return to the Bible as a reference book. Will our children or their children recognize when politicians borrow powerful phrases from the Bible without attribution?

Jonathan Aitken wrote in *The American Spectator* (March 2011) about the hundreds of common expressions that have been traced back to the 400-year-old King James version of the Bible. The key word, in my opinion, was "common" expressions." Common to whom? *National Geographic* magazine, in December 2011, also had a cover story article on the impact, import and influence of the 400-year-old Bible translation.

Many good and great political speeches have biblical references but no direct attribution, so people now may not recognize their original sources other than from the speech giver. This 400th anniversary has caught the attention of many other publications.

Some common biblical expressions listed are fly in the ointment, my brother's keeper, fight the good fight, finding the scapegoat, how the mighty have fallen, bricks without straw, new wine in old bottles, blind leading the blind, root and branch, turning the other cheek, scales falling from eyes, holier than thou, going the second mile, reaping the whirlwind, fall by the wayside, sour grapes, two-edged sword, old wives' tales, and writing on the wall.

Since I am a political junkie, I thought about certain realities in politics that are best described in biblical terms: "30 pieces of silver" and Pontius Pilate's "washing his hands" after his decision. But other cultures/religions also have expressions no longer understood by younger people. I referenced "no sacred cows" once at a meeting of volunteers for a town event. My daughter pulled me aside to let me know that people had no idea as to what I was referring. As the world gets smaller with technology and communication, it will become a necessity to have a better understanding of religious and cultural differences.

While the demographics of this country are changing, will we forget the significance of our Judeo-Christian heritage, including language? While many have walked away from mainstream churches, as evidenced by declining church attendance, we were nonetheless grounded first — before we may have decided to walk away. Have we forgotten that our children and their children may still need to have an understanding of our culture and our collective history? It is the grounding in Western civilization now that seems to be missing.

Think of the many eras of heavy immigration, such as after the Irish Potato Famine. With so many Americans claiming Irish history — even Barack Obama — it may be hard to imagine that there was great resentment against the Irish in the 19th and into the early 20th centuries. America has been called the "melting pot" of the world. As a foodie, I like that metaphor and it is timely, because we are seeing a cuisine fusion across this country from all our different sub-cultures, creating new and popular dishes.

As to our humanity, I once heard the late John Silber 1926-2012), former president of Boston University, say that all we need to know about ourselves can be learned from the history of the Peloponnesian War, about 400 years B.C. or B.C.E. The B.C. initials told me as a child that the time period was measured before the birth of Christ. The B.C.E designation now refers to a time period "before the common era." The ancient Greek stories tell of greed, alliances (hmmm; the enemy of my enemy is my friend), money, power, plague, population changes, romance and powerful Navies.

Many people did not like Silber and that was very evident when he came before my regional school committee. John had a short-term reign as the head of Massachusetts' schools. The man did not tolerate fools. He was prophetic in calling for a return to classical education. If it is good enough for private schools, why not let public schools use a classic education model as one option too?

While I am focusing on elementary and secondary education, it was interesting to read in *The Wall Street Journal*, September 3, 2010, that Columbia University was bucking the college trend and returning to a core curriculum based on the "great books of Western Civilization."

Young children can also benefit from classical Greek myths: think of "Pandora's Box," "King Midas," "Echo and Narcissus." I found a Usborne (Educational Development Corp.) book, *Greek Myths*, just a perfect way to introduce mythology to children.

However, our favorite Greek book is one my family found at our local dump "library" exchange, a small wooden shed at the transfer station for trash that allows people to recycle books and help themselves to others. It was there that I found D'Aulaires' *Book of Greek Myths*. The book had belonged to a teacher's son. I took it home.

At age 11, my granddaughter needed physical therapy for her eyes. She really detested doing the daily exercises. She asked me to read to her to help pass the time. It was this book of Greek myths that I chose to read. She enjoyed the stories and became fascinated with Greece. That year, in sixth grade, she chose to write her country project about Greece, both current and ancient.

My point is that when we read to children, we never know where and when an interest may be sparked or how it will grow. My granddaughter attended a private school for 7th grade where she thoroughly enjoyed a semester reading translated ancient Greek stories.

Human traits, for better or worse, are timeless. The reason to read biblical or ancient Greek stories is to help us understand our humanity. Every story — biblical, ancient history, current-day — has a physical setting. The tie-in between geography and so-called bible studies is intrinsically interwoven to that story's place and time — as are all aspects of education.

What stories do you want your children to know? I see a great void now regarding older, more historic, and especially biblical stories of history, but I am hopeful that those who pass on stories will be providing shape and direction for our children and that we will remember and pass on the stories that helped shape us, too.

When we were children, if an adult caught us doing anything wrong, we would probably hear "You should be ashamed of yourself." To me, the absolutely scary thing today is that too many children have no concept of shame, and how could they? Think of all the outrageous behaviors that kids see these days on TV. With little to no parenting, many children have no moral compasses to guide them.

It will be the stories we tell to our children that can shape their characters, introduce values and link them to us.

Do you think the Vandals and Visigoths are at our city gates? What stories do you value? What stories do you want your children to know to take with them into adulthood, so that they have them in memory, to take or leave as they make their own decisions, which they will, undoubtedly? What value do you place on rituals, family, religion, secular understanding and sports? What rituals, if any, would you choose for your family? For a start, what do you think about your family sitting together, enjoying pancakes and one another's company for breakfast on the weekend?

"America is not like a blanket – one piece of unbroken cloth, the same color, the same texture, the same size. America is more like a quilt – many patches, many pieces, many colors, many sizes, all woven and held together by a common thread."
— Jesse Jackson in his address to the Democratic National Convention in San Francisco, July 17, 1984

"Smart is an elusive concept. There is a certain sharpness, an ability to absorb new facts. To ask an insightful question. To relate to domains that may not seem connected at first. A certain creativity that allows people to be effective."
—*Bill Gates, founder of Microsoft*

Chapter Four

School Stupid but Street Smart

Today educators talk about "multiple intelligences" and "differentiated learning." I do not want to get caught up with jargon or theories. I am not convinced, however, that our schools recognize many hands-on type of intelligence. I think grandparents recognize that each grandchild is different in every way, including how each learns and what are each child's inherent abilities. How does that recognition occur in schools?

Even at an elementary level, we do not seem to recognize the abilities or learning styles of each child. For many years, I read to second graders. What a delightful age but also, for some, a very sad time. It is sad because most of the children, whatever their abilities, start to recognize ability differences among themselves. This is particularly true when it comes to reading. Children will and do know when their peers are reading and they are not.

One year I was reading a Judy Bloom book chosen because the setting was in a big city, New York City. I would generally have from zero to 10% (or one) of the students who had been to New York

City, which is about 200 miles away. In our Victorian-era village, we do not have tall buildings. I needed to expand their concept of housing to include high-rise apartment buildings. We discussed living in an apartment building that could be taller than the mountain behind our school and have elevators to move people from floor to floor and that many buildings in New York City have more residents than we do in the whole town. For most of my students in many ways New York City is a foreign country, so I take the students on a trip in their minds. For instance, in the "A to Z Mystery Series," in the "J is for Jaguar" story, the characters go to a Japanese restaurant and so we went to a Japanese restaurant in New York City where our main characters ate seaweed. Of course second graders true to form did a collective, "yuck."

One day's reading had the briefest of mentions about drug problems in Central Park and parents not allowing their children in the park at certain times of the day. My students knew that I expected them to raise their hands with a question if they did not understand a word or what was being said. That announcement is made at the beginning of the year when I introduce myself. I also let them know that asking a question is a sign of great intelligence and that probably others have the same question. While reading the Bloom book, a child raised his hand to ask what a particular drug reference meant. Suddenly a little girl is just about jumping out of her skin, hopping around, shaking her head, saying, "I know, I know."

Sadly, I'm thinking, "Of course, you do." This is one of the hazards of living in a small town. I knew her family's history. I also did not want this situation to be her moment to shine in front of her classmates. I quickly smiled and told the child that I had it. I kept my response brief and honest, as that is all that is generally needed with children, and proceded with the story. As with any awkward situation in the classroom, I told the teacher about it before I left in case there was any further mention of it.

But I thought about this later. How is it that some of our children can learn all the nasty things of life and then fail in school? If they have street smarts, are they not capable of much more? If they can learn about the local drug trade, they can learn other things also.

I remember the first time I heard that expression "street smarts." The occasion was my Mother defending a child who did not like school but was a very capable amateur mechanic. She acknowledged that he was smart, but in a different way. My Mother referred to people who could learn outside of a school setting without books as having "street smarts." Even with his mother's support, the child came to think he was stupid when he was growing up. I am using the word "stupid" in a colloquial sense.

The description of a different kind of ability was not original to my Mother. We were fortunate to have two very intelligent parents who quite casually and conversationally shared ideas with us. As I look back, I understand how my parents were what we call "life-long learners" today. Long before the general public was talking about chemical imbalances in brains causing inappropriate behaviors, my Mother had made that observation, for example. I find myself recalling many of her thoughts as I write this book.

My late brother Jimmy always hated school, did not like to read and constantly struggled to simply pass each year. But my Mother insisted that he finish high school. With that accomplished, he was soon drafted for service in Vietnam. Perhaps had he been in a community college doing remedial work, he might have been spared that experience, but he would be the first to tell you how proud he was of his time in the Army. From being a grunt (private first class) initially, he was quickly promoted to sergeant and then captain of his Army boat during his nineteen months of military service. Initially, his tour of duty in Vietnam was for one year, however, if you signed up for an additional month in Vietnam, you eliminated any remaining stateside duty. I cite his choice only for the purpose of explaining how quickly he moved within the ranks. He was one of the "river rats" delivering ammunition and supplies along various rivers in southeast Asia.

This story is relevant to this book because we can learn from the military. The various branches of our armed services have proven track records, honed from years of experience, to recognize skills, particularly leadership. Have you ever observed natural leadership abilities in any group situation? My brother had that natural ability. He only talked about Vietnam late in his life. After I became an EMT in my town, he told me how he designed an emergency helicopter landing on top of his boat. He was a "river rat," performing some of the most difficult and dangerous assignments, and yet he jury rigged a solution to fix a problem that was not per code or in any manual.

He returned from Vietnam to the United States at a time of great civil protest but uncalled for disrespect to anyone in uniform. He said he wanted a white-collar job, as he never wanted to experience that kind of disrespect ever again. Fortunately his family reminded him of his vast talents with automobiles. Jimmy bought his first car at the age of thirteen for $10. He started "tinkering" with cars and that passion became his livelihood. He had his own successful auto collision and repair shop. He was such a car fanatic. His work was also his hobby. He loved creating custom cars. In 1978, he took the "Best Truck" award nationally with "Fury," a custom truck he created at the International Car Association U.S. convention in Las Vegas. I remember seeing a 1934 Ford in his garage that he chopped down into a roadster with a custom paint job of black cherry, a beautiful new interior and re-built motor. My nephew was young at the time but he has such fond memories of that vehicle in the Philadelphia World of Wheels car show. Then-children's TV personality Captain Kangaroo recorded a special TV show about that event and featured "Bad 34," my brother's car.

Even when his health deteriorated after life-long complications from Agent Orange my brother could still paint a steady, straight pin stripe on a vehicle. His childhood hobby became a financially rewarding vocation. Now his son's goal is to recreate similar memories for his child. How great is that? But my brother would not have been considered successful by school standards. With each year's growing success while still a young man, he finally shed that destructive self-image of being stupid.

A more contemporary example is a young friend of mine. As is the custom here in rural western Massachusetts, when he was ready to build his barn, his friends and neighbors all arrived to help. Most came with their own tools. One man happened to be an engineer. He asked to see the plans for the building of the barn. My young friend picked a scrap piece of 2x2' lumber and, with his carpenter's pencil, made a simple outline sketch of what he wanted the barn to be.

All heads nodded with an innate understanding and the ballet began. I say ballet because from a distance that is how it looked – completely coordinated and silently orchestrated. That barn today is a visual asset on the scenic Mohawk Trail.

The "how" of learning or teaching has seen many changes but some elements of learning are constant. An older friend told me about his youth in Hell's Kitchen in New York City. In his multi-ethnic neighborhood, kids learned, for example, to swear in many other languages. In many ways that is similar to children growing up in bi-lingual households. They can easily learn more than one language if they are exposed to other languages. And yet, most schools still introduce foreign languages in the middle or high school, when many kids then struggle. This debate has been going on for a very long time, depending where you may be in this country.

I know of a school that is finally using the Rosetta Stone Language Program, a self-learning program now available electronically. I recall Rosetta Stone's advertisements in *National Geographic* magazine in the 1950s, when the program was on LP (long playing) records. It was promoted then for adults to learn another language for business, travel or diplomatic purposes.

Why am I mentioning this? It is a fact now that our children are learning how to learn at their own paces because they will be doing that their whole lives with all the technological and other rapid change occurring in every field of work.

This particular school decided that a teacher would be needed to use this program with students. I think the educational community may not realize how adept kids are with technology on their own. The Rosetta Stone Program does not require supervision. I was distressed to hear a school leader's comment that not all children are motivated when I asked for a progress report. After a few months, I asked the new young Spanish teacher how it was going – in an Ed Koch manner. Ed had been a mayor of New York from 1978 to 1989. He was known for approaching his constituents on the street and asking, "How am I doing?"

The teacher's response was most interesting. "Many are struggling and need a lot of supervision," he said. That made me wonder about the earlier "motivation" comment, so I asked, "Why is that?"

"Well, if they are not good readers, they struggle," was the response. So this had absolutely nothing to do with motivation. Then why do so many school problems seem inevitably to go back to poor reading and the child gets the blame?

I am pleased that the new leadership is applying more challenges to students, but low expectations frequently pop up. I see a correlation between the poverty rate, limited enrichment experiences and low expectations that creates a self-fulfilling scenario. I contend that "street smarts" is one barometer of ability, but also a base upon which to build. No matter what age a child comes to school, I think it is crucial that all focus be on reading if the child is behind the eight ball, otherwise he or she will self-label as stupid. It is not the school's job to make a child love to read but to read at a minimum level to perform even minimal work.

If a child has difficulty reading directions, for example, he starts to assume that he is stupid. This is how the self-fulfilling nature of this problem builds on itself and compounds. The child also sees that he is not reading as his peers are reading. It is a heart ache when you hear a child label herself as stupid. This happens. You may want to debate the frequency, but that is not the point. The light goes out of a child's eyes when she cannot do what her classmates appear to do seamlessly.

It becomes almost impossible to change the child's self-image as a learner when this happens. It can be done, but only with a lot of effort and a teacher or other adult working with the child. Sylvan Learning TV ads actually are a prime example of showing a child's frustration. Except for those with severe learning disabilities, children can learn to read, however, if we wait too long to identify struggling readers, we may cause irreparable damage. Most debates about education revolve around what we must do to improve high schools. That is too late. The tenor and tone of the child's education for all intents is set around learning to read by second grade.

If a child at the age of three does not know the front of a book from the back, she has not been exposed to books. This is a child who starts school at a great disadvantage. What assessments are made to address this deficiency? I am not advocating spending a lot of money on specialized tests. The simple observation of how a child holds a book is a major clue.

Nothing else matters in these early years at school except reading. The child may be a good artist, dancer, fixer, athlete, or musician but he or she will and must have a basic reading level. How many times have you heard other adults say that they are not readers?

The name of the game is to have children reading, because no matter what their interests or future work, they will need minimal reading skills. Please note my use of the word "minimal." This is not an argument to lower standards. This is a demand that every child leave elementary school with at least a minimum reading level of grade five. If we did that, perhaps we would have a lower dropout rate, fewer behavioral problems in middle and high school and fewer frustrated students. It takes a highly motivated middle school student to increase and/ or improve a reading level; actually that is an oxymoron. The child with reading difficulties is not unmotivated; he is beyond discouraged. No child should get to that point. It is our responsibility to stop this now so that hands-on learners are not handicapped in the future.

Hands-on abilities are areas that can be fostered, encouraged or promoted at home. "Tinkers" are people who just seem to know how to fix or make things. Do you know a jack-of-all-trades? Is this avenue one that might lead a grandchild into successful self-employment? Did you hate school yourself? Did the class reading out loud drive you nuts? Did the school reading books have boring stories? How will you recognize, help and promote a child's abilities, whatever kind?

Does your family have a "street smart child?" What interests him? How can you help with that interest? For example, when my 10-year-old son suddenly had no interest in reading, I found *Guitar* magazine, since he had become hyper-focused on music. It has been my experience that every interest has a magazine, e-zine or Web site catering to that interest.

Have you thought about ways to help a child access basic reading material that complements the child's interest? How can you offset the boring books in school that are some adult's idea of what kids like? Who knows if your basement or garage will produce the next Steve Jobs? Or will your guidance lead a child to pursue her passion that possibly enables her to be self-employed?

"It's really hard to design products by focus groups. A lot of times, people don't know what they want until you show it to them."
— Steve Jobs, Business Week, May 25, 1998

"Only the curious will learn and only the resolute overcome the obstacles to learning. The quest quotient has always excited me more than the intelligence quotient."
— Eugene S. Wilson,
Dean of Admissions, Amherst College,
Reader's Digest, April 1968

Chapter Five

Pygmalion in the Classroom

I am of an age that I write with great familiarity of the 1950s and 1960s and I see that as a distinct advantage. I am able to remember when I was my granddaughter's age. If I should forget anything or embellish a detail, I am blessed with a life-long friend who feels free to correct adjusted memories!

In September 1963, I started my senior year at Bishop McDevitt High School in Wyncote, PA. The school is located in Montgomery County just across the Philadelphia city line.

Within our school's student population, there was only one sending-city parish elementary school, but all other parishes' schools were from Montgomery County. In terms of demographics then, we were a suburban, middle-class school, full of the new generation of so-called Baby Boomers, with parents who came of age during World War II, the majority of whom made their big move from the city to the new suburbs. For reference, think of the stereotypical Levittown of the 1950s. While my generation came later to disparage what we called

the ticky-tacky nature of those developments, I now
know how blessed we were in our childhoods. As
young children, prior to high school, we raced home
from school to go outside to play – unsupervised.

But with one parish in the city I had the opportunity
to see a little bit of city living other than visiting my
paternal grandmother in South Philly. The easy
access to buses and trolleys that ran frequently and
reliably enabled us to move about when we were
not walking. In the city you could walk to almost
anything you needed. My new high school friend
Carolyn introduced me to a Jewish deli in her
neighborhood. I have been a foodie my whole life
and that deli was my first memorable food
experience beyond my Dad's awesome cooking.

When we arrived for our senior year of high school,
we found a major change at our school. Previously
the girls' teaching staff was comprised of three
orders of teaching nuns.

Note that I referred to the girls' teaching staff. That
is because in those days we had the girls' and boys'
sides of the building. Today it co-ed. Recently I
spoke with three A/P English classes there about
writing. I started each class with a comment of how
weird it felt to be on the boys' side of the building.
A young teacher said to me that my comment
explained to her why the center of the building had
two staircases. The school has been co-ed for so
long that some of its history is being forgotten.

I mention this not as a trivial point but as a sidebar.

Many now attribute single sex education as a good foundation regarding women of my age for future leadership roles. As I told the young women at McDevitt in the spring of 2011, we did not have to worry about looking too smart in front of boys because they were not in classes with us. Hillary Clinton credited her education at Wellesley College, a girls' school then (1969) as her part of her start in leadership roles.

But this new, fourth order of nuns, The Grey Nuns of the Sacred Heart, were not only an addition to staff but, we soon found out, a force for change.

In our senior year, some of our classes were not tracked or ability-grouped. Prior to that, we were either in college preparatory or business school classes, in three tiers by abilities. I had, until then, always been in top tier classes in high school. Our untracked class that year was history with Sister Mary Eleanor, one of the new nuns. What a character in every sense of that word's permutations. She was so different from anything we had ever known in a classroom. She actually wanted to know what we thought. That was a novel concept at that time.

I can vividly recall Sister Eleanor asking Melly (Mary Ellen) what she thought about something. The something part I have long forgotten but I do remember turning in my seat as Melly started speaking. I was so shocked. You see, I had known Melly since third grade. Melly and her siblings played with me and my siblings. Melly stuttered. Then it was understood by us as kids that stuttering was equated with being dumb even though my

Mother told us it was not true. If you have not seen the 2010 movie "The King's Speech," I recommend it as a good reference on a general attitude on stuttering in the 1940s and 1950s. Not only did Melly speak in Sister Eleanor's class, she had something interesting to say. Again, I don't remember her words, only that I was so impressed and interested.

Then in 1968, when I already had two children, I read a book review in *Time* magazine on *Pygmalion in the Classroom* by Harvard professor Dr. Robert Rosenthal. I quickly realized that this simple concept of believing in the ability of every child and having them reach higher standards was exactly what Sister Eleanor had employed in her classroom.

I wrote a letter (pen to paper) to Sister Eleanor. I told her of the book review and my realization about her teaching prowess. Sister wrote back that she was familiar with the book and technique from her own studies. Most of our teachers always attended summer school classes. We actually had brilliant women teaching us.

This is all so pertinent today as we constantly talk about improving education. Dr. Rosenthal believed that "expectations influence performance." Another way of expressing this was done by President George W. Bush in 2004 when he referred to "the soft bigotry of low expectations."

Recently I received an e-mail containing a YouTube video of small, kindergarten-age Chinese students playing classical, acoustical guitars. I forwarded this video to my local elementary school principal with a note: "Our kids will have to compete with these children in just a few years."

President Barack Obama has now on several occasions spoken about the need to compete in an ever-more competitive world marketplace. If your own elementary school does not believe in competition and challenging students, you may see your child being stifled. This is where you can start to see philosophical and political differences among schools. For example, do you know how your family's school feels about competition?

For the purposes of this book, I am using the categories employed in MCAS (Massachusetts Comprehensive Assessment Systems) of Failing, Needs Improvement, Proficient, and Advanced.

Think about this example in a small, rural elementary school: The class size is twelve students; four are Advanced; two, Failing; six, Needs Improvement.

Can you think of anyway you can present one level of material to such a diverse group? What generally happens is that the most common denominator is used. Schools may say that they use differentiated teaching, but if this is a new issue to you, it is imperative to question the teacher about the class make-up and how he o r she addresses those differences.

While we may want to avoid the "soft bigotry of low expectations," we also do not want, at an early age, to reduce our expectations for our brightest or best-prepared students. Boredom can lead to behavior problems in a classroom. Or worse — the child gets the wrong message; that it is okay if something is good enough or it does not matter.

Good enough never is whether you are a doctor or a home improvement contractor. I am suggesting a re-thinking about standards and the subliminal messages we send to our children.

I recently tracked down Melly living in Alaska, where she has been for 40 years. Her comments about Sister Eleanor were powerful to me because she so vividly remembered that Sister really was interested in what her students had to say. That is empowering to students but also concrete evidence that after all these years, the teacher's actions are remembered for their impact.

What will your children or grandchildren remember 40 years from now?

Maybe this is all about expectations.

I know of a young woman who became a teacher because of a dreadful early elementary experience. She was very quiet and shy. She was placed in a lower ability group until in fourth grade a teacher recognized her abilities and she was moved into a higher group. Her memory is distinctly then having to play catch-up. She taught herself the multiplication tables. I do believe there is a connection there as she is now a fourth-grade teacher. Her passion is that no child should ever feel as she did in her early school years when her teachers had low expectations.

She has high expectations. In her teaching career, I have seen this young woman perform "Hamlet" with fourth graders when everyone said it was not possible. But she had been given Charles and Mary Lamb's *Tales from Shakespeare* as a child and that secured her enjoyment of Shakespeare before arriving in high school. So she did the same with her class. A Shakespearian play became an after-school project with practices and, finally, a production before the whole school.

This same teacher befriended a high school science teacher, another mother attending soccer games for their daughters. In the course of a fall season, they decided it might be a good idea to bring the fourth graders to the high school as a class to see the high school science fair. The superintendent approved a bus for a mid-day trip from one school to another. The high school students particularly enjoyed discussing their own projects with the young ones.

In another time and era when large families were more prevalent, this kind of sharing was done within families. If anyone doubts this sharing and learning among siblings, ask any mother with two children how much more quickly the second child will be able to do anything. The second child is like a mirror to the first and not at all afraid to try something that an older child is doing.

But from that visit to the high school, the teacher took her usual fish unit and expanded it into a mini-science fair hosted by her fourth-grade class in small teams. The fourth graders imitated their new, older friends with poster boards of research and a fish tank. Each team had a hypothesis. They stood proudly before their work and talked about their research to younger students – third graders.

These students now own that knowledge but also see science in a new, confident light.

I want to make a final note about Pygmalion and self-fulfilling prophecies. When I returned to McDevitt recently, I wrote to the president of the school afterwards with some of my impressions. The strongest impression was so different from the principal's comments to me about the school's diversity.

When I attended McDevitt, it was an all-white school with two black students. From just my visual observation, the school now appears to be 50% white, 40% black and 10% Asian. For those who like more categories, I would note from accents I heard in the halls, that there were island blacks, Central Americans, Koreans, Chinese, and Vietnamese. My point is a lot of diversity, as it is measured these days.

However, what struck me though was how middle class the students all appeared. I live in an area with free- and reduced lunch program numbers generally at 50%. I have seen how different low income and middle-class income behaviors can be. I know that there are many students at McDevitt receiving scholarships based on financial need but there is, nonetheless, an expectation of middle-class behaviors and standards. It was absolutely striking for me to see.

I feel we are now so afraid to appear judgmental in anyway that anything goes – good, bad or indifferent. Perhaps others with more fineness can approach this issue of class-associated behavior. I am merely calling attention to the issue. If this is an issue where you live, how will you deal with class behavior differences? What children see on a daily basis becomes their reality.

I have seen some parents called "elitist" by educators when they seek higher expectations. I guess the educators attribute that to a perceived insensitivity to others' perhaps lack of resources when actually, it is an attitude of expectation versus little or no expectation. It is not related to income level or resources. For me a good barometer might be if you get verbally attacked or severely criticized for wanting more, it might be time to look for alternatives because of low expectations.

Consider the Harlem Success Academy, which came out of the charter school movement and where there is an expectation that every child can succeed. We need more models such as that.

What choices are you able to make on schools where your family lives and how will that affect expectations?

While I write about choices in general, I do want to ask political and educational leaders why vouchers can not be given in urban areas for Catholic schools, particularly if they consistently have better results? Former Los Angeles Mayor Richard Riordan points to a 98% graduation rate for LA's Catholic schools. What urban public school system has a graduation rate even close to that, even if you adjust for other factors? The debate about vouches generally revolves around whether they help all students, yet there is no evidence that vouchers harm any students. Is it time to stop arguing about all students and allow parents to choose for their children?

The Wall Street Journal on October 1, 2011 had a headline: "The Latest Crime Wave: Sending Your Child to a Better School." An Ohio mother was charged initially with two felony counts for using her father's address so she could enroll her children in a better school. We should consider that a wake-up call. School districts will not verify if children are legal residents but school districts across the country are hiring special investigators to verify true home residences.

Truth is stranger than fiction.

This is the only chapter where I mention Catholic schools, however, there is another point to be made here. When I visited my old high school that was built in 1962, I was in awe of the physical condition of the building. While improvements, such as new energy-efficient windows, had been installed, the stairwells still had the original tiled walls with no cracks and the original mortar. Why does this matter? What does it mean?

The work was done with pride. Children, also, over the years were taught to respect the property. Our teachers told us at that time of the sacrifices our families made to build our schools. We understood the concept of stewardship.

That is not always the case with our public schools. I happen to find that insulting to the taxpayers who have paid dearly for public schools. The difference with private schools is that students are more aware of sacrifices made on their behalf. Additionally, life is messy at times so we all need to know how to clean up after ourselves. A local, private, non-religious school has a weekly rotation of chores for all faculty and students to perform.

What can you expect from your local school? Does it meet your expectations? Is your child challenged with expectations? Do you have choices? Is the monolithic public education system the only choice where you live? Would choices through a voucher system offer needed competition and a better education for your family?

"In automobile terms, the child supplies the power but the parents have to do the steering."
— Dr. Benjamin Spock in Ladies Home Journal, March 1960

"Perhaps it is the specter that haunts working men and women: the planned obsolescence of people that is of a piece with the planned obsolescence of the things they make. Or sell."
— Studs Terkel, 1972

Chapter Six

Get a Job!

As children we were told that if we graduated from a catholic high school in Philadelphia, we were guaranteed to get a job! Prospective employers knew we had a work ethnic. I know it was a long time ago. Also, I certainly do understand the differences between then and now, such as the decline in manufacturing jobs and the growth in technology jobs. This is not a sign of old age but a challenge to schools to produce workers.

Yes, I used the word "workers."

The first point to be made is our children from an early age need to be taught about working, even those going onto four-year colleges and beyond those who ordinarily think of themselves as careerists or professionals, not workers.

Work skills are developed and refined from a very early age. Setting the kitchen table for dinner is an appropriate chore — aka, work — for very young children. Consider this a mini lesson in teamwork. Learning how to cook with family members takes an everyday chore and turns it into a special time. Using your Dad's recipe for a particular kind of gravy, while explaining the details to the next generation, becomes a storytelling time. It also is one of those steps we encourage our children to take towards self-sufficiency.

I know this from my own memories at home as a child when Dad was preparing family feasts for various holidays. My father was the great cook in our home. Our mother attempted to convince us that burnt food was good for us. She had many great talents but cooking was not one of them when we were younger. As she got older, she had the time to practice and did eventually become rather good. But Dad was a natural. He lived to see the beginning of the "fusion food movement," however, he knew instinctively how to mix and blend flavors. There was nothing bland in our diet. In high school one of my surprises was that not everyone ate as well as we did. By well I am not talking about cost, but his ability to draw out flavors with even inexpensive foods and to provide variety.

I have tried always to do the same with my own family. When my grand daughter was 18 months old I would put her in a backpack contraption on my back when I was cooking.

She would peek over my shoulder and I would explain sautéing, frying, mashing. I just talked through the details of what I was doing. True to form, as an older child, she wanted to do it herself. She saw cooking as a fun activity and naturally gravitated to cooking and enjoying good food and her own creations.

I know I make many food connections and it is for a variety of valid reasons, one of which is finding common ground. I have heard many employers complain about the absence of common sense, initiative, self-direction and overall work skills in young people. Cooking with kids is an opportunity to introduce the idea that when they grow up, move out, find their own places to live and get jobs, that they will also have to feed themselves in a healthy fashion. Yet, for many, this may seem archaic. I find today's discussions about the costs of living seem to miss setting priorities. An extreme example might be the 25-35-year-old living at home, maybe even in a converted basement apartment, because he or she spends so much on expensive electronic toys and games that he cannot afford to pay rent. What I am seeing is that some people are not able to distinguish between necessities and discretionary expenses. Learning to set priorities on spending can be — and used to be — taught at home at a young age.

Cooking is part of maintaining yourself – being self-sufficient and even healthy. Perhaps a small part of the American obesity problem can be traced to a real change in our eating habits. Between prepared foods and fast foods we can see a definite correlation with obesity. There seems to be a disconnection between us and our food. By that I mean we are buying and using more and more prepared foods that only need re-heating or a quick nuke in the microwave.

I was asked a few years ago to go into a second-grade classroom early in the morning to offer baking lessons during choice time. The teacher and

I brought in the needed supplies and cooking/baking equipment. We had an arrangement with our school cafeteria to bake. The children, supervised, would deliver the item to be baked along with the instructions for time and temperature.

Sounds like a fun activity, doesn't it?

Well, actually it was a math lesson in measurements. The majority of children did not know what baking was. This became a lesson plan around measuring spoons and fractions thereof (1/8-, ¼-, ½-teaspoons), multiplication (4 tsp. = 1 tbs.) The same was true for various-sized mixing bowls and measuring cups in U.S. customary or metric system of measurements.

Okay, maybe you are fortunate and live in the metropolitan Philadelphia area where real bakeries still exist and thus have no need to bake. But do you want your younger family members to know how to make pancakes on a weekend morning? How will they feed themselves when they go out on their own?

This kind of initiative is what employers say is missing in young employees. I understand that former President Bill Clinton did say that "every" child has the right to go to college." That is not going to happen because most of our students do not have the skills for college work. The highest college graduation rate for states that I have seen is 35%.

What is happening to the other 65%?

I think about the WWII generation, sometimes for inspiration but also as examples. Our world with all its technologies is different but our humanity is not.

My Dad left high school in March of his senior year with parental permission to join the Navy at age 17 just a few months after the bombing of Pearl Harbor. I have also thought of George H.W. Bush volunteering at age 17 and then at age 18, becoming a pilot. Truth be told, their training as pilots was short and brief as they were put into the skies generally with only three months' training. They were able to do whatever was needed of them at that time.

During that time what was needed was quick, fast, innovative responses to workplace needs. "Necessity is the mother of invention" alternately contributed to Aesop, Plato, Ben Franklin, however, it is a concept still needed as we compete in a world marketplace. Then and now we need people who are resourceful and able to do whatever is needed of them. Work then was a means to an end. Rosie the Riveter was not looking for personal fulfillment. She worked to fill a need. Bruce Springsteen's song "Factory" is from the perspective of Baby Boomers, but the World War II generation did not expect self-fulfillment. However, recently I needed a telephone repair that turned out to be a line problem on the street. I asked this pleasant person why he liked his job. His response was, "It's always different with lots of challenges . . .and I am not like the recent grads carrying huge college debt while looking for jobs in this time."

In 1974, Studds Terkel wrote the book *Working* that greatly influenced my thinking about working. The man's intense respect for all kinds of work came through loud and clear. I was working as a waitress in 1976 to pay for my college tuition at UMass/Boston. It was while waiting on tables that I had another very important learning experience that I did not understand until many years later. I have come to understand Plato's idea that potential leaders should do manual work as the final part of their training before becoming leaders. He thought a future leader should put in five years working in a salt mine after all education before assuming any leadership. I think six months of waitressing would have a similar tempering effect today.

Somehow, somewhere along the way in my lifetime we have come to hold a college degree so high in value that there was an unintentional diminishment of work per se, yet, we all need cars maintained, electricians on occasion, plumbers when a pipe leaks, our trash picked up, houses painted, driveways plowed in a snowstorm, waitresses to serve food, beekeepers to make honey, etc.

While my neighbor built his sugar house himself, he is a minority in knowing how to build anything. It is not just building or making anything anymore. In my sister's development, a local handy man is paid $65 an hour to make minor repairs or perform simple tasks that nonetheless require tools, such as hanging pictures. Only one generation ago the Power Company could and did hire 18-year-olds right out of a high school because their fathers taught them a wide range of skills, including basic electrical skills. Today, the same entry-level job requires certification before hiring. U.S. manufacturing work is now 10% brawn and 90% brains, as opposed to the old ratio of 80% brawn and 20% brains.

The majority of our students will need skills and work habits. It is time to talk about that.

In education, I think all too often we see young people being directed to college when maybe initial talks should be around work. Sometimes guidance counselors forget that most people work to live; while a smaller group lives to work. This is not a subtle difference. It is real and needs discussion. Also, I heard a sentiment recently that probably is the quiet truth about American high schools. A community leader expressed his opinion that if the top 20% are doing well, then the school is a success. That, I realized, is the cultural bias that we do not discuss publicly.

Starting with the work concept is also a time to teach and show pride in workmanship. Doing any job well is an important character trait. I think it starts at home but schools can emphasize the value of neatness, for example, in any written or printed assignment. What impression do we want people to have of our work? Are wrinkled papers indicative of not caring enough to store the work neatly in a binder?

I cringe when I hear the expression "Good enough." I find "good enough" never is. Why?

"Husbandry" is a lost word that may be making a comeback, as my granddaughter told me it is a term used in her environmental science class. However, living in a rural area I have actual examples of husbandry in its original meaning of thrifty management of domestic affairs in farming. Hayfields trimmed neatly versus sloppy cutting shows one's pride in workmanship. But, included in that definition is the word "thrift" that is different from cutting corners on a project. My neighbor recently built his own sugar house to make maple syrup as his son wanted to try it. A good example of being thrifty was his use of old windows in construction of the sugar shack. Making maple syrup is a very labor-intensive activity that once started, requires round-the-clock work to completion. You are stoking the fire every 15 minutes, watching the flow of the sap into the evaporator, stirring and skimming off any foam, keeping an eye on the thermometer. But the most important element to this process is a father working with a son to continue a New England tradition in their personal life classroom. This son knows the value of good work because his father has taught him.

We all recognize when someone gives a 100% versus 50%. After Hurricane Irene in 2011, parts of New England experienced horrific flooding. Swollen rivers swept up all kinds of debris — natural and man-made — that littered riverbanks and fields. Trees ripped from riverbanks could be found after the storm jammed in standing trees about eight to ten feet off the ground. So far, only one area has been cleaned up. It is a family farm along the river that is a perfect contemporary example of good husbandry. The care they give their farm is now a visible example to others.

This is a great conversation starter in school or around the dinner table. The point is with little ones and young children you are planting seeds, such as, "when you grow up and get a job . . .bosses like people who do their work well, neatly, and timely." Employers say it is difficult to find reliable and dependable workers. It is your conversations and stories with your children or grandchildren that will determine their direction and whether it reflects your values.

When did we stop talking about work? It is a natural course of events. It is part of our socialization. Work is not necessarily a 9-5 situation, either. Earlier I wrote that some work to live. By that I mean with the salary from a job, after living expenses, some can use discretionary income to pursue their interests or hobbies.

While writing this book, I came across an article in a July 2011 *Ladies Home Journal* titled, "Want to be Happier?" Do things by hand and your brain will thank you, because working with your hands can flood your brain with natural antidepressants. For me, knitting, quilting and gardening are ways for me to work with my hands. What do you do? What can you teach your family to do? Boredom for children today is a dangerous thing. Perhaps a little manual work in their lives might lead to contentment? Perhaps for working parents, a child's chores can contribute to the overall smooth running of a household. At some point, earlier is better. Children need to know that life is messy; clean it up. It seems at times that we have become disconnected from our own humanity. Learning to work and take care of ourselves is part of our humanity. If you doubt that, talk with a person who has been laid off recently.

My personal example of a working man is our local school custodian. It is so apparent, if you look, to see the pride the man takes in his work. When you walk into the custodian's room, with his supplies adjacent to the boiler room, you see organization with meticulous attention to detail. His workspace also mirrors his home workshop. He is consistent in his attention to detail. The orderliness is a pleasure to observe. To his chagrin, a school building committee in its renovation plan, included white but slightly speckled floor tiles. The old buildings were dark, dank and depressing. It was not unreasonable that the teachers wanted light and bright colors. But as with everything in life, there was also another perspective held by the school janitor.

Think of how kids' sneakers make black scuffmarks. After expressing his dissatisfaction with me, he resolved the problem. He took mop handles and added a tennis ball on the end to create a perfect buffer to remove the marks. But what pleases me most is that our students take turns using Mr. D's invention to clear the hallway of scuffmarks every morning before classes begin.

How do you involve children in small chores? What ways do you think you can teach personal and community responsibility? What behaviors do you show to your younger family members? How do you discuss work? Is this discussion even needed?

I communicate with many teachers of all ages in multiple ways. Recently a Generation X teacher told me of her plans to attend a two-day seminar about effective techniques for teaching reading. Sometimes I am not clear with my choice of words, which happened when I asked, "what difference will this make?" The teacher said she found that once a year to leave your classroom to go to a seminar offers influences, inspiration and invigoration by being with fellow professionals and, sometimes, you learn something. I asked again but with more details, "what difference will this make on your students?"

"None," she said, "as they do not see any relevance to hard work." Then after a pregnant pause, "as none of my students have working parents."

None! This group of parents includes two-parent households also with no one employed. The teacher said, "it is as if I told my children to brush their teeth everyday but I never did it myself."

This Great Recession impacts aside, the change in the number of adults not working has long-term consequences for all of us. How is that teacher supposed to teach children, expect them to do their "work" as students, when the concept of work has no meaning for them? One teacher with no students having a working parent may be an anomaly or the beginning of another decline in our society. What do you think is a tipping point? What do you expect teachers to be able to accomplish with such constraints?

When we were children, we were able to have a swim club membership because our father worked to obtain that membership. He found out that he could work every Sunday in the spring helping to prepare the club for summer opening to get that family membership. He had one full time job, plus a part-time Saturday night bartending job, but he worked another job for us to have that opportunity. When I was raising my own family, people, including me, would also take seasonal, part-time jobs before the holidays to buy toys and other gifts for children. This was before credit cards and today's crushing consumer debt.

I am grateful for three very practical gifts from my parents: resourcefulness, creativity and excellent working habits. However, they were not simply handed to me. My parents taught us.

"The chief cause of problems is solutions."
— Eric Severeid, Readers' Digest, March 1974

"No job, no money, no marriage,
No kids, can't keep a car
educated to be a slave."
— "Parva Que Sou (What a Fool am I),"
sung by Ana Bacalhau of the band Deolinda,
the lament of a generation (in Portugal), 2011

Chapter Seven

When You Go to College . . .

Since my first granddaughter was born in the 1990s, our family has made references to when she goes to college. It is a matter of setting up expectations. Recently, the same child, now in high school, asked me if she could have my small electric teapot when she goes to college! For her, it is a given that she will go to college. Our expectation now is her realty.

A broader, less personalized example might be the 1998 animated movie "Antz" with Woody Allen as the voice of the neurotic ant who did not want to be a worker ant. He actually thought and verbalized to his therapist that there should be more to life for him. An even more contemporary animated film is the 2007 "Bee" with Jerry Seinfeld's character who also wanted more . . . the more being undefined.

What do you hope for your child? Within our country's collective memory parents, have sought better lives for their children. Every immigrant family — whether 150 years ago or now — makes sacrifices so children will have better lives. What is considered "better" is very subjective and not always what a child may want. Do you have your own immigrant family story to share? What does your family consider the "good life?"

As our nation's immigrant family members sought a better life, so, too, is that story playing out around the world. If sub-titles do not bother you, I would recommend a Chinese DVD called "Last Train Home" by Lixin Fan (2011). Even without sound, you can understand the plot. It recounts the story of one family among the 130 million Chinese migrant workers who take the train home once a year to see their families during the Chinese New Year holidays. They have gone to the big cities to work in manufacturing to earn money to support children at home being raised by grandparents. With all their sacrifices nonetheless, a daughter drops out of school to earn her own money working in a factory also The last scene shows the daughter as she is walking down the street with her stylish, skimpy, slick clothes, heading off to a nightclub to swing and play and not think about tomorrow's factory work.

Our collective humanity as parents and grandparents is competing with very strong social and seductive forces. A very clear example is the larger society's inability to distinguish between wants and needs. This also leads to incorrect solutions, if a problem is not understood. Self-esteem for a child living in poverty can put the horse before the cart. We must understand what motivates us as human beings. Abraham Maslow (1908-1970) created a chart around his findings on human motivation, a hierarchy of needs. The following chart, typically shown as a triangle, should be read from the bottom up:

Self-Actualization
Personal growth and fulfillment

Esteem Needs
Achievement, status

Belongingness
Family, affection, relationships, work groups

Safety Needs
Protection, security, order, law, stability

Biological and Physiological Needs
Basic life supports – air, water, food, shelter, warmth, sex, sleep

This has significant importance to education. For example, a teacher with a child in an unsafe situation, such as domestic violence, or without basic needs, such as sufficient food, will not have the full attention of the child, nor is the child able to fully concentrate. More on this in other chapters, but for the purposes of this chapter, how do expectations start?

When my children were small, I took them to our local children's library, a small, white, clapboard, old house converted into a children's library. It was adjacent but separate from the town library. My kids were registered and understood the procedures. They knew where to place the books they were returning. They could walk around, find their own selections, and then go to the checkout desk. There they kept the children's library card on file. The child only had to give their name.

One day we drove there and I told my daughter that she could go in by herself. I reminded her of the procedures. We assured her that her father would wait in the car while I went into the big library. I quickly obtained what I wanted and returned to the car. Within twenty minutes or so she returned to the car. The child was absolutely beaming as she skipped to the car! Our five-year-old said to us, "I felt like a six-year-old!"

When my kids were preteens, occasionally they would accompany me to downtown Boston where I was a day student at UMass. I allowed them to take the subway unsupervised to Cambridge (to a music store). I explained how to read the signs in the subway, gave them a return time, and let them go.

This is not suggesting that my way would be the best for readers' families; I am giving two examples. How and when will you start to teach your children or grandchildren to fly on their own with confidence?

Many people work to live on weekends. That is fine, if they find work that pays for a particular lifestyle. However, some live to work. Happy is the person who loves what he or she does. This is true for degreed occupations and others. Work can be a means to an end, or the end itself.

I always think of Guy Fieri of the television Food Network when looking for a good example of a person happy in his work. He is one happy man. His work is about food and all its pleasures. He seeks out unusual places in out-of-the-way diners, dives and drive-ins. I happen to challenge my normally aging brain by writing occasional sonnets. This is my sonnet to Guy:

Guy Fieri Sonnet

Diners, Drive-ins and Dives, foodies' road trip
Guy (Fee-eddy) takes us on a food fling
With spikes of hair, Hawaiian shirts, and flop flips
Some tats, in shorts, great shades and Jersey bling.

With the top down cruising open road ways
In his convertible all shiny red
North, South, East, West along the old blue
highways
Towns, off the beaten path, where folks are fed.

With long lines out front to savor,
Salivating and anticipating
Real food, fresh not frozen, local flavor
Sometimes, surprise fusions, new tastes creating.

Guy loves his cool Diners, Drive-ins and Dives
Originals all that deserve high fives.

I could discuss Guy in the previous chapter as well as here. The point is that discussions about work as a means of initially supporting yourself are more effective if started early in life. As I wrote in the Preface, do you want your child to be a drone or make her own choice? That choice on how to support herself can include fun, interesting or soul-satisfying endeavors.

There are two additional aspects about Guy that have direct correlations to educating a child. Guy, also, has another show on the Food Network called "Guy's Big Bite," where he frequently includes his young son. He has him chopping, measuring and doing actual work himself. This is a good demonstration of how kids like to do almost anything if you let them.

Secondly, on Guy's 3 D's show I have been impressed with the entrepreneurial spirit of the small but awesome restaurants that he visits. You can watch the pride with which these cooks, chefs and grandmas have in their work. Whether it is Cuban, Vietnamese, Italian, German, Bar-be-cue, Southern, Tex-Mex, or fascinating fusions of food, these folks are creating delicious food. As Guy says, "these people are the real deal." Restaurants are one of the most challenging and difficult businesses to operate. First of all, your customers will expect consistency in the food and the service. This is where knowledge and work habits meet.

I am a very practical person. That said, I would suggest that expectations go both ways. For the average American family paying for college, there might be an expectation of getting a job after school. Esoteric degrees for many are not worth the cost, either the immediate job prospects or long-term debt to the student or family. I use the term esoteric in the sense that it has no value in the marketplace; its value is with only a chosen few. If you are independently wealthy, of course you may study for the sheer pleasure of it, but I am not responsible for that debt. Other than for the wealthy, this is an example where decisions could be based on Maslow's *Hierarchy of Needs*. If a senior graduating from high school has no idea of what he might be able or want to do, then perhaps we might look to the Israelis with a two-year, mandatory military service or you might direct a student to a service-based community organization. We do not necessarily need a national service when there are already so many organizations needing help.

How will your family help your child to choose a meaningful gap activity, if that is appropriate? After that period of service when young people approach college, they are serious students. Additionally, in job interviews after collage graduation, they offer more real-life experiences of working with others, having maturity, and even possessing leadership skills that employers are seeking. What would you suggest to a child in your family who needs a gap year or two before college? Sometimes by having a gap year the student is actually able to finish college in four years as opposed to five or more. The next financial crisis has already been identified: huge college loans.

This worldwide Great Recession has many pausing, perhaps even thinking anew. Jobs that once required only a high school diploma now need an associate or full-time degree. Does the degree signify an acquired skill level or is it something else? Is there a correlation in the shift from hard science degrees to the soft sciences, such as math versus economics? Or physics versus paleontology?

I first heard the sad song from Portugal at the head of this chapter on NPR with a lead-in of "How

Dumb Am I?" In this country, we are seeing over-educated baristas making coffee or other overly priced foodstuff. Unless you are independently wealthy, it is time to evaluate a degree upon its earning value. Then, on your own time and dime, anyone can pursue additional studies, such as Russian Literature. In the 1990s, I met so many young geeks and nerds in high school who taught themselves all about computers. Steve Jobs was not the only bright person to question the value versus the cost of college.

Our country is seeing a so-called shortage of middle-level skills that require additional schoolwork after high school. That is receiving a lot of attention now along with funding from the federal and state governments. Those programs lead to employment. If you cannot afford to extend your child's childhood, how will you prepare him for the real world?

Expectations as a high standard must work with realistic goals. I wonder where were the adults in students' lives who allowed or enabled them to take on such debt as reported by the Occupy Wall Streeters. I wondered when the housing bubble first burst in 2008, when the evening news showed a bus driver losing her $750,000 home in Los Vegas due to an adjustment in the terms of the loan. Did she not wonder how her salary would work with that debt? So from ignorance, stupidity and greed the house of cards fell. When political leaders say that every child has the right to go to school, qualified or not, is it because we have empty classrooms to fill? The "business" of college has become separated from the original intent of colleges and universities.

When you go to college it is an extension of your work as a child in elementary and high school to do the work in a timely fashion, finish and join the real world where you are expected to pay your own bills.

"Life comes before literature, as the material always comes before the work. The hills are full of marble before the world blooms with statues."
— Phillips Brooks (1835-1893)

"In the realm of ideas it is better to let the mood sally forth, even if some precious preconceptions suffer a mauling."
— Robert F. Goheen, President,
Princeton Commencement Address,
The New York Times, June 19, 1966

Chapter Eight

My Hero, Albert Shanker

For many years the late Albert Shanker, a past president of the American Federation of Teachers Union, had a weekly column that appeared across this nation in major newspapers as a paid advertisement. If my memory serves correctly, I started reading him occasionally in my 30s during the 1970s. That is not a math quiz; it is a frame of reference.

His common sense appealed to me. When I became a school committee member in the mid-1990s, I sometimes quoted him. But he was no longer a known figure or maybe his columns never appeared in this area. So much information is available these days, perhaps it may be difficult to comprehend small but significant differences between major metropolitan areas and really rural areas before the Internet. Rural isolation has become almost a thing of the past, however, there are still far too many areas without broadband service. Yes, there is dial-up, but who seriously considers that as connected? As rural electrification changed this country, so could a commitment to complete Internet access. While our public schools have full high-speed

Internet access, most of the area's residents do not. From my perspective, this is one of several major reasons why old, rural New England towns are losing populations. For those with access, the world is at our fingertips. And, as with everything else in life, it has its upsides and downsides.

Marshall McLuhan coined the expression "the global village" when he was writing in the mid-late-1960s. He introduced the idea of the medium (electric technology) that was reshaping our social interdependence. Prior to the Internet is an interesting earlier example of an older medium and its social impact: radio. I was initially confounded to find that this area, the very northwest corner of Massachusetts, had a healthy fan base for the New York Yankees. "What's with that?" I asked. I guess I just assumed that this would be Boston Red Sox territory. The explanation came one day at the meat counter at Avery's General Store. The banter was about the Yankees from a woman who clearly loved baseball. I expressed my surprise at her being a Yankee fan and asked "how come?" Debbie explained to me that there was a radio tower on top of nearby Mount Greylock in North Adams, MA and you could hear the Yankees games broadcasted from New York. You could not get Boston radio in this area then.

Also I was told that there was basically no TV here in the late 1940s and early 1950s. However, asking around I found that one household did have a TV in 1952. Situated on a high point in this village of Charlemont, that home's antennae provided limited access. A teacher, Thelma Purinton, arranged to take her 4th-, 5th-, and 6th-grade classes to Henry and

Franny Avery's home to watch the inauguration of Presidential inauguration of Dwight D. Eisenhower. Of course, the students were expected to behave properly while there and, upon returning to school, to answer questions about what they saw.

While doing local research I heard many interesting stories. If you were very lucky and the weather was cooperating, you might pick up one TV station in Schenectady, NY from an antennae mounted on your roof — unless your house was at a low point or blocked by the mountain. Forget about rabbit ears, as they would not work.

In addition to limited radio, so it was with newspapers. The news tended to be local or regional. This is not just a trip down memory lane. With this hindsight, we can understand now the changes and impacts we have seen in our lifetimes and will continue to see. All changes bring elements of good and bad. We can and do have choices to make as we use all available means of media. Current technology by HD satellite transmissions now allows live performances from the New York Metropolitan Opera to the rural, enchanting 1897 Memorial Hall in downtown Shelburne Falls. As the world gets smaller, our opportunities are enlarging at an exponential rate.

For this book, I knew my memory alone would not suffice to write about one of Shanker's columns. I Googled the union's name, found an e-mail address, wrote requesting the column called "A Million Drowning Children" and within hours received an e-mail reply with the column attached. What a world we now inhabit!

I received *The New York Times* copy of the June 6, 1993 column. I had read it in the weekly edition of *The Washington Post,* now defunct. The following is the entire paid advertisement:

> Irving Harris, the well-known businessman, philanthropist, and child advocate, tells a parable about some people picnicking beside a river. Suddenly they see an enormous number of babies being carried down the river by the current. Their first impulse is to jump in and pull out as many of the babies as possible. But the kids keep coming, and the rescuers can't save them all. Finally, someone is smart enough to run up the river to see who is pushing them in.
>
> Like most parables, this is rich in meaning. But Harris intends it as a comment on the way we handle the problem of disadvantaged children – particularly those born to unmarried mothers who may not have wanted them in the first place and who don't give them the nurturing children need. Our primary intervention is the education system. In "Education – Does It Make A Difference When You Start?" (*Aspen Quarterly*, Spring 1993), and in an even more hard-hitting speech, "Primary Prevention vs. Intervention," Harris calls this too little, too late.
>
> Harris points out that as we spend a great deal on education. Yet even middle-class children do not achieve at the same levels as youngsters in other industrialized countries, and disadvantaged children do much worse. In some cities, half the students drop out, and many who graduate don't have the skills to get a decent job or to benefit from college.

We hear many ideas about how to help the education system succeed with these youngsters. But even if we gave schools every imaginable resource, Harris says, it would still be like jumping into the water to save kids who are already drowning. We must go on trying, but we are kidding ourselves if we think that improving K-12 education is enough to solve the problem.

Research shows that the brain develops most rapidly during a child's first years. Babies who don't get the food and health care they need are likely to be slow to develop and may be permanently harmed — long before they are old enough to enroll in Head Start. Harris cites a study that found an astonishing 12% of preschoolers to be learning impaired because of preventable causes like malnutrition, lead poisoning and neglect.

But a child's physical well being is not the only issue. Babies need parents who make them feel secure and loved, and "a poor, single mother — especially a teen mother — who starts off with low self-esteem and lacks security… may find it difficult to teach the baby, through consistent caring and interaction, that the baby is safe and loved." Youngsters who do not get this nurturing are likely to enter kindergarten unprepared — and begin a spiral of failure that lasts throughout their school careers and beyond.

These poor kids are not the only ones who pay for their lack of readiness. The kindergarten teachers Harris talked to said they could handle one such child without "shortchanging" the others, but that if they had more than one, the learning of every child in the class suffered. This means we have an enormous national problem.

In 1999, 29% of American babies — more than one million —were born to unmarried women, many of whom were children themselves and had no job and no understanding of what it means to raise a child. By 1995, the figure will be one-third. In how many classrooms will all the children suffer because one child is not ready?

As important as education is, it cannot take the place of social policy in dealing with a million drowning children. There are people who will strongly disagree with Harris's Plan, but his analysis of the problem — and of what we face if we don't deal with it — demands everyone's attention.

Shanker wrote these words in 1993. Irving Harris, who helped create Yale's Child Study Center, died in 2004. In the Congressional Record (House, Page H7585) of September 28, 2004, then Congressman Richard Durbin wrote of Harris, saying, "Kindergarten is much too late to worry if a child is ready to learn. We must begin in the first days and weeks and months of life to get children ready to learn."

What will be our tipping point as a society when we are ready to analyze the problem of neglected children AND simultaneously admit the schools cannot fix this?

Shanker used the words of another to make his point. Probably about ten years ago I rhetorically asked the question, where is the line between neglect and out-right abuse? I raised the question in conjunction with my opposition to school breakfast.

100

I wondered if an adult was unable to get a bowl of cold cereal and milk ready in the morning for a young child, what else was not being done? Perhaps I framed the question directly and too strongly, but it is time to ask these questions because life is becoming more difficult for our children.

In 2010, 22 states accepted federal grants to offer school dinner under the Healthy, Hunger-Free Kids' Act. Does anyone else see a pattern here? We seem to just add more programs without identifying all the parameters of a problem.

My mistake may have been in attempting to draw a line between neglect and abuse, but lack of nurturing or neglect is quite damaging in the first three years of life. And what is the solution to that problem? Do you think mandatory pre-school for four year olds will address these problems or deficiencies? I agree with Irving Harris. He wrote his parable in 1993. Now it is 2011 and our numbers seem to be getting worse. While social change is like a ship, slow to change course, we are almost through another generation of too many lost children.

In his article, he mentioned a teacher who said she could handle one such ill-prepared child but anymore would change the dynamics of the classroom in a negative way.

I have a life-long, dear friend who has retired as a public school teacher. For more than 40 years I have seen changes in this person. This wonderful teacher always gave 110%, was always studying and taking classes herself, was open and receptive to innovation and completely believed in the power of education. She has now chosen to teach only one graduate class a year to people who want to learn. Just in case I didn't understand what she meant by that, she clarified: she does not want to be with or deal with anyone who does not want to learn, do the work, be on time, know how to write, and attend all classes.

I have watched this heart rendering change from eternal hopefulness and optimism to a sense of hopelessness about our educational institutions. I have seen others engage in passive/aggressive behaviors when some new program, superintendent or school committee dictates to seasoned teachers to lower their standards. This is what Harris meant by his kindergarten teacher's example of her accommodation.

My admiration for Mr. Shanker is primarily based on his expressing direct opinions. He was not universally loved for his opinions, though. We force leaders to speak Pablum so as to not offend anyone; therein may lay our problem. Joel Klein, a former New York City Schools' chancellor, has been quoted quoting Albert Shanker, "when school children start paying union dues, that's when I'll start representing the interests of school children," when speaking to the power of the teachers' unions. While grateful for his "million drowning babies," I have no allusions as to his viewpoint overall.

Evaluation and accountability are long overdue from all concerned. Whenever a child arrives at a public school at the age of three, four, five or six, depending upon parents' choices, we should establish a baseline of that child's abilities. From that point, it is the school's responsibility to show improvement and advancement only based on the initial input. This measurement has nothing to do with a grade level. If the child arrives ready to learn, the child will learn quickly and in an age-appropriate manner; if the child has been neglected, the progress will be slower and smaller. A baseline should also be established when a child enters a new school as a transfer student, so we can gauge fairly teacher performance.

Evaluation and accountability are long overdue for both families and teachers. I no longer accept a statement made to me by an elementary principal: if we don't do it, who will?" The "it" in that not very logical statement is for the myriad services now performed by schools: two to three meals a day; supplying clothing; providing after-school care and medical care, on top of the various state mandated services. With all these efforts, the results have gotten proportionately worse.

This is not to hurt children or to take food from them. It is a call to rescue the million drowning babies. Providing more services has not worked. When you see a TV ad that refers to one in four children going to bed hungry, it is true. Our grand plans are not working. Even taking care of all the basic needs for far too many, there are still children who do not have food in sufficient amounts, or safety and security in their lives.

Regularly scheduled evaluations of staff and programs with accountability might have avoided the exponential growth in childhood poverty. The institutionalization of education has made it moribund, stagnant, and inflexible to any change that does not match that frame of reference. Harris had it correct. It is time to review social policy with all its negative, unintended consequences.

What are your expectations for professional behaviors of teachers? School committees? Superintendents? State Departments of Education? How often are teachers evaluated? With so many teachers in my family, I am biased in favor of teachers. But I am also an advocate of merit pay based on extraordinary work. Ordinary work done well and each child showing measurable progress are two suggested parameters.

What expectations might we have of parents? If a child leaves second grade in June at a 2.3 reading level but returns in September with a level of 1.9, who is responsible for that? If schools provide three meals a day Monday through Friday but the child is not fed over the weekend, who is responsible for that?

The unintended consequences of good intentions are damaging children and future generations. Who should address these problems? Should schools' primary mission be returned to education? Building onto existing programs, spending more money and not correctly identifying the scope and nature of our problems are not viable choices. Mr. Shanker had great courage in writing that piece on a million drowning babies 20 years ago; now it is a matter of admitting a mistake and fixing it . . . ourselves.

What can you do as an individual or as a member of a group?

"We have inadvertently designed a system in which being good at what you do as a teacher is not formally rewarded, while being poor at what you do is seldom corrected nor penalized."
— Eliot Eisner, professor Stanford School of Education, The New York Times, September 3, 1985

"Only the curious will learn and only the resolute overcome the obstacles to learning. The quest quotient has always excited me more than the intelligence quotient."
— Eugene S. Wilson,
Dean of Admissions, Amherst College,
Reader's Digest, April 1968

Chapter Nine

Teachable Moments

In Chapter Two, I gave an example of a teachable moment where the teacher asked each student to look inside of their sneakers to see where they were made.

How open to do you see your local school to teachable moments? A problem with a statewide curriculum and testing is that sometimes we can inadvertently be stifling our best and brightest teachers. No, wait; as I type those words, I know I am wrong. The great teachers will always find ways to teach to the best of their ability regardless of imposed regulations on them. The majority, as a majority in any group, will not engage in a lot of thinking on their own. That is perhaps the yin and yang of groups. State-directed curriculum frameworks are meant to be an outline of the subject matter covered. It is not meant to restrict how the subject is taught.

In my childhood, we were taught civics. Included in that material was how our government was

structured with the Solomon-like task of balancing
the rights of the individual versus the larger society.
It is easy to point to extreme societies that do not
have individual rights as measured against our
democratic republic with a constitution. Yet our
society is constantly dealing with the natural
tensions inherent in our system. People in groups,
without any constraints, have the human tendency
to become tyrannical or, at a minimum,
institutionalized. An example of that is manifested
in the movie "Dr. Zhivago." Recall, if you will, the
house commissar informing the original owners of
the house that their personal space was again going
to be reduced, or Dickens' Madame Defarge
knitting while watching the executions during the
first French Revolution, or the metaphorical pigs in
Animal Farm. I have a personal bias against large
groups. I happen to like people. I just think that
people get funny sometimes in an unpleasant way
when in groups.

Regardless of state directives, the thoughtful
individual teacher will make connections with the
knowledge she has to impart that leaves a real
impression on students. It seems sometimes that we
have separated our children from the world in which
they live. All too frequently students do not see the
relevancy of subject matter.

The day of the Chilean mine rescue of 33 men from
2,000 feet below the Earth's surface after 69 days of
entombment with an American-made drill was
absolutely inspiring on many levels of human
emotion. I discovered later that there was no
mention of it at my local high school. I did have an
opportunity to discuss the rescue with two young

people. One of them happened at one time to live in Brisbane, AZ. Her immediate reaction was, "I'll never work in a mine," based on her own personal observation and discussion with those who worked in mines there. She related to us how hard the work was. The rescue held relevance for this person.

That rescue was a teachable moment. Besides American technology, the Japanese, South Koreans and Germans contributed to this rescue. *The Christian Science Monitor* reported the operation as an "engineering showcase." The drill bit weighed 13 tons! We desperately need more engineers in this country. Could this have been a five-minute news report in a math class that would have shown real-life application of engineering principles?

Did your family discuss this rescue? This can happen sitting around a dinner table, hanging out on a basketball court, taking a walk, cleaning a garage, driving around, or texting. A conversation on the rescue could have been your moment to teach a family member.

Also, schools could have used this for a discussion of cooperation amongst nations. Smartplanet.com reported that the rescue was possible [because] of innovative companies from across the globe. The event was described in terms of parallel significance to the Apollo moon landing.

There are additional science examples, such as NASA's high-calorie drink that kept miners from getting sick while the rescue capsule had to rotate 10-12 times in the 28" diameter escape route.

Or a journalism class could look at how the rescue was covered around the globe. Al Jazeera News reported in the old Joe Friday fashion with just simple facts. CBS News reported that the rescue capsule was dubbed the Phoenix 1 and used that name to explain the significance of the mythical bird and how it arose from the ashes to new life.

I would suggest for middle and high schools an occasional five-minute news report would be in order, however, I actually do understand schools' time constraints and priorities. With all the mandates, it sometimes seems that the curriculum is a mile wide but only a half-inch deep. To get around time constraints, perhaps a history teacher could require a written paragraph on a daily basis of something in the news (TV, newsprint, online, tweets, etc.) that relates to their class subject area. I actually had a teacher who had this requirement in my senior year of high school but it was from newspapers.

Spices, seasonings and herbs add depth to your cooking. How can you add depth to your child's education? If this is not done in your school, do you think as your child's first teachers that you might discuss current events with him or her?

The rescue of the miners was not boring. It captured the imaginations of many – just not enough children, I fear. Will our children be ready for the world they will be entering in a few years if they know very little about it?

When I worked in the corporate world, the Communications Department had a "clipping service" that sent photocopies of pertinent news articles to the appropriate department needing that information. Now with technology, anyone can read anything and almost immediately forward to others with a similar interest or need for the information. When I do it with my immediate family members, I call it M-M's Continuing Education Service.

Knowledge is power. How can you enable your children with knowledge you find invaluable? What skills do you want to pass along that may enrich your child's life? How can you use a teachable moment with your children?

In the previous chapter, I wrote about a teacher taking her class to the only TV in town to watch a presidential inauguration. Thelma recognized a teachable moment. She is still remembered fondly by students she taught in the 1940s and 1950s, but she is also recalled as very demanding with high expectations. I have the personal pleasure of being friends with two of her grandsons who also are contributing, productive residents of our area.

Teachable moments are similar to throwing pebbles into a pond. Watch the reverberations with expanding circles of influence.

"[It was] an initiation into the love of learning, of learning how to learn, that was revealed to me by my BLS masters as a matter of interdisciplinary cognition – that is, learning to know something by its relation to something else."
— Leonard Bernstein, on the Boston Latin School,
The New York Times, November 22, 1984

"Few things are harder to put up with than the
annoyance of a good example."
— Mark Twain, 1894

Chapter Ten

The 3Rs versus the 3Ds

A hundred years ago school discussions revolved
around the 3Rs – reading, (w)riting, (a)rithmetic.
Now I think of schools within the larger educational
community as imperious. Anyone who questions,
let alone challenges, schools find him or herself
probably subject to the 3Ds —diminishment,
demonization and demagoguery. These tactics
effectively stifle debate because discussion is cut
short. I think these three actions have directly
contributed to the changes in our cultural and
political discussions. First, I probably should define
discussion: talking and/or writing in which the pros
and cons of a subject are considered. Nowhere do
you see the definition saying one side or the other is
right, correct or the only allowable opinion.

Anyone who raises his or her voice with a
difference is quickly smacked down. This is not a
personal rant (although I am able to cite same), but I
am able to hold my own. I think my point can best
be made by citing Bill Cosby's experiences as I
have observed through multiple sources of news
reporting on his "Come on, People" book and
speaking tour.

Mr. Cosby has always been known for his humor. Before he became a national figure, he started in the city of Philadelphia. I even can recall one of his first comedy acts on TV in which he imitates a young boy playing a submarine submersion by flushing of the toilet tank with the lid off. A teenager myself at the time, I thought he captured the essence of small boys. On that I am expert, as I had six younger brothers.

Mr. Cosby is too big a persona to be diminished. He cannot be demonized because he and wife do many, many good works in multiple areas of giving, including education.

However, experts called him a demagogue during his book tour in 2007. There was a hint of what was to come in 2005 on the 50th anniversary of Brown vs. Board of Education in a speech to the NAACP. Cosby dared to speak off message in a very politically incorrect way. If you need to see how he was vilified, Google "criticism of Bill Cosby." Various reports in numerous ways said directly that he exhibited classist behavior. He was even accused of failing in his duties as a racial representative. The worst criticisms the media or social critics can throw at anyone are "classist" and "elitist." Once one is so labeled, he automatically seems to lose credibility to speak, particularly about education.

Most of the criticism was directed against Cosby's person, not his points of disagreement. I read where people loved his humor but did not like him as a "scold." I remember similar disapprovals of Jimmy Carter's Sweater Speech in 1977. In that speech, he suggested that Americans turn down their home thermometers one degree (to save oil) and, if cold, put on sweaters.

I am a New Englander by osmosis and time. We tend to be a frugal, hearty and resourceful people although historically, we are not the only ones. I recall growing up that my grandmother kept a "house" sweater. It was an old, tattered, stained sweater not suitable for public showing but quite suitable to wear in the house if she were chilly. Now if a grandchild of mine says, "turn up the heat," I say, "get your house sweatshirt." If that makes me a scold, so be it.

When anyone group can determine who can speak or what the parameters of a debate are allowed to be, we no longer have discussions or debates. Because Cosby has achieved great social and economic class, he is not permitted to speak on so-called black issues unless he follows a proscribed message although, to his credit, he continues with his own message.

Where I live, half of our students eat free- and reduced-priced lunches. That is the number and measure used by schools and governmental agencies to gauge poverty. I have personally seen a middle-class woman called an elitist because she is able to spend a lot of time with her boys and — wait for it — told it is not fair to other students whose parent or parents have not done the same. This class warfare is so destructive, but also a guarantee that there will be no escape from lower-class poverty. It is behavior that will define class.

What behaviors do you see in your school(s) in this matter? For example, is there a code of conduct? I suspect you will see that code includes personal responsibilities for students. Are all students expected to be personally responsible? Or do you hear excuses about why some children have behavior problems?

Is your school community open to real discussion? Will you be called an elitist for wanting high standards in reading, such that every child (short of the severely learning disabled) leaves an elementary school with a minimal level of skill with reading at the fifth-grade level? Are children allowed and encouraged to achieve their highest reading levels? Does your school allow a child to use software whereby he or she progresses at her own pace, even if she passes her peers?

When anyone is mocked, humiliated or otherwise hurt for daring to question, eventually none of us is safe. What choices do you have when a monolithic group determines it knows more than you do about your child? With political bullying, is it any surprise that we see a rise in the number of Mean Girls? What will happen to your family if you think differently than the majority?

Have you ever seen humor used to diminish a person or a question? Have you ever seen or heard someone described only in very nasty terms if he questions the status quo?

"All truth passes through three stages. First, it is ridiculed. Then it is violently opposed. And then it is accepted as self-evident."
— Arthur Shopenhauer, German philosopher
(1788-1860)

*"Habit is a cable; we weave a thread of it each
day, and at last we cannot break it."*
— Horace Mann (1796-1859)

Chapter Eleven

Horace Mann's Leadership

Writing, thinking, and sometimes daydreaming, I
am looking out the window of my study to catch the
long view up my valley that is filled with glorious,
great greens in June. From the field grasses to the
mountains' trees, it is nature's tapestry at its best,
except, possibly in the fall. I live in the rural,
northwest corner of Massachusetts. In the 1990s,
Channel 5, WCVB TV-Boston's "Chronicle"
program, aired a show about this area entitled "The
Land Time Forgot."

So much about education is written from an urban
perspective. However, I bring an additional
perspective to the table for discussion. The
Commonwealth of Massachusetts has an early and
long history in public education starting in 1837
with the appointment of the first Secretary of the
State Board of Education, Horace Mann. Mann is
frequently referred to as the Father of American
Education or sometimes, the Father of the Common
School.

I became intrigued by Mann when I came across his
name in "Charlemont Massachusetts 1765-1965
Bicentennial History" by Allan Healy written in
1986. I was writing a white paper, "The Funding of

Massachusetts' Rural Schools" at the time, 2003, to lobby the legislature in Boston. I generally look behind me to see what was or proposed in the past when analyzing contemporary problems.

The early one-room schoolhouses now do not seem archaic, as they strike me as a possible model for future use here in New England with the world available to all with Internet access. That idea is not original to me, as western states first proposed it more than 15 years ago. There are huge transportation costs associated with regional school districts. One argument, of several, for regionalization was to reduce costs, but the increased costs of transportation challenge that reality. Also we are seeing major shifts in our nation's demographics with an increasing numbers of retirees. It is the declining enrollment numbers of elementary schools in New England and Rust Belt states that also contribute to the increasing costs of education.

In the late 1800s and early 1900s, several of the area's so-called hilltowns in western Massachusetts built high schools with classical curricula, complete with student plays, music and sports. Each town's history reveals a strong commitment — financially and otherwise — to public education. The schools were the heart of many towns.

In Healy's book, he wrote, "throughout the years, Charlemont played host in its schools to many teachers' institutes and meetings. In 1847, for instance, Horace Mann (as the education secretary), called an institute (think conference) in Charlemont for the meeting of teachers who were instructed to bring their own bible, pen, ink, slate (as in stone) and pencil, and a geography, an atlas, and the reading book most used by their highest class, together with a dictionary and a blank book for notes."

Obviously there is a little humor for us today with certain words, such as slate, pen, ink and I guess some would think of a "tablet" as an "iPad" instead of a blank book for notes. To me the most significant part of that statement is "the reading book most used by their **highest** class."

First of all, it is an acknowledgement that there were class rankings. Mann has been called the Father of the Common School but those words had a different meaning then. Today, common generally means the lowest common denominator. That would be contrary to Mann's stated belief that the common school would be the "great equalizer" in that even the poorest of children could succeed in school.

In this area during town meeting, a forum open to any registered voter, school budgets are voted as a lump sum with no provision to change anything within the budget. Recently my own school system, in a handout for town meeting, noted some educational highlights; one referred to "Tiered Instruction (Response to Intervention) – Increases differentiated instruction and academic achievement."

Would it help if I translate that? It is a reference to ability grouping. There is now an understanding and acceptance that we need some ability grouping to effectively teach to those who need remedial work versus more challenging work. It only took 15 years with the efforts of many who were, at times, called elitists for resisting the custom of each child reading the same page of the same book. Imagine a child who was able to read all the then-available Harry Potter books being told he had to participate in a third grade class's reading book. Behavior problems can develop when an advanced student becomes bored.

Horace Mann understood that it is the challenging work that will bring others up also. That is the very reason he wanted to see the reading book used by the highest class. Those who have raised two or more children have probably seen how the second child generally copies the older sibling and seems to do everything earlier than the first child. This is not complicated. I encourage young mothers to trust their instincts with their children. If you see signs of boredom even in kindergarten, ask for more challenging work before your child gets the wrong message. Or leave that system, if you are able. Or speak to your school committee. Or get thee and thine to a library quickly to augment the child's interests. Or go on the Internet, but find interesting, challenging materials to keep the child interested in learning.

Mann also thought that education would eradicate poverty. Almost two hundred years later that is still true for education itself but not always as it is happening in so many of our schools. If we measure the poverty of children, according to TV public service announcements, one in four children go to bed at night hungry. Childhood poverty was very real even before 2008. But with the on-going Recession of 2008, it appears to be more prevalent nationally.

I do not want to think of a child being hungry. I also understand why school personnel, with their great caring hearts, can justify almost anything to help children.

My preference, though, would be to feed children and simultaneously determine why they are hungry. That children were hungry was the impetus for school lunches on a free- and reduced-cost basis. Then here in Massachusetts in the 1990s, schools started breakfasts because children were coming to school hungry. Since 2010, with the Healthy, Hunger-Free Kids' Grant, all states are accepting grants to provide school dinners.

Does anyone else see a pattern? If Albert Shanker were alive, I wonder how he would see this? If schools continue to provide solutions without correctly identifying the problem, is it unreasonable to wonder what is next after school dinners? I think at times that there is a fine line between neglect and abuse but I do wonder if no one is able to put out cereal with cold milk in the morning, what else is not being done for the child.

We cannot afford to label anyone as judgmental for asking these types of questions, yet that does happen — more often than we realize.

At one point I wondered if we were headed back to the colonial concept of a "poor farm," "almshouse," or "poor house" contained within our schools.

Those institutions all declined by the mid-1900s as they were replaced by welfare. So, now with welfare in place, we are not eliminating poverty programs, we are adding more programs at our schools to address the growing number of children needing nurturing.

We are familiar with each generation of the last hundred years with defining characteristics that distinguish them from one another, however, each generation is always convinced of its own invincibility. The Boomers were so arrogant in the 1970s when we suggested "trust no one over 30." We also thought that the Great Society would end poverty. If current measures are any indicator, not only have we failed in our efforts, is it time to ask if our current education system is indirectly contributing to the problem? How have we come to see the third generation in poverty depending upon governmental assistance in this area? So often these types of discussions revolve around anonymous populations. In this general area, these observations are closer to the ground. Historically there have always been working poor in this area but the dynamics have changed. We still have working poor, some of whom even own their own homes. Any kind of manual work that needs to be done has kept them employed year-round plowing snow, mowing lawns, cleaning houses, house painting, gardening, whatever-ing. Welfare debit cards and our own state's housing policy that in essence requires all cities and towns in the commonwealth to offer 10% approved and designated low-income housing have created a real divide.

Housing is one of those issues affecting education. I even understand what the stated goals were as to every town having low-income housing — and then there are the realities of the consequences. Spreading around the low-income housing without regard to the exiting working poor, transportation availability, health care facilities and employment opportunities tends to lead to the law of unintended consequences.

During the confirmation hearings for Judge Sotomoyer much was made of her being raised by her widowed mother in a low-income housing project in the Bronx. What was not included in any of those news reports was the additional piece of information that totally changes that report. Those projects, built post-Depression and during WWII, were for working families. Boston also had similar projects. A dear friend grew up in a Charlestown Project. Her parents moved there in 1939. This was housing for the "respectable, working poor" to help them get back on their feet.

My friend and I recently discussed this aspect of low-income housing. We both had housing courses in our schoolwork at UMass. In those early days of public housing, there was no requirement on the number of bedrooms. In contrast, today a single mother, one son and one daughter would necessitate a three-bedroom apartment versus in her day as a youngster, when there would be multiple bunk beds to accommodate large families. And, it was not unheard of then for parents to sleep on a pullout couch.

Those details, "working families," are in most cases missing today. Words do matter. Except for a widow, a family included a mother and father. While we talk about the increasing number of children growing up in poverty, we also do not mention that about one-half of our nation's children live in single-parent households. There is a connection.

Some might call that previous paragraph judgmental. I do not want to tell anyone how to live, however, our national changing demographics have meant a lack of parenting for far too many children. That does have a real impact on our schools.

Have we created a permanent underclass? Will 10% unemployment be the new norm? I think there are connections and, as always, the laws of unintended consequences. But if we cannot talk about this, it will simply continue to get worse. I think it quite reasonable, after all these years of society experimentation, to ask why is education not eradicating poverty?

A third rail in education I have found is Head Start.

Woe unto she who challenges that, however. (Go to the government Web site for a clear example of "obfuscation.") Yes, Head Start does have measurable results in the first year or two and that is how the report is written. But the benefits are only temporary and disappear with each passing year to zero by high school. Why are they not permanent? If it does not change the child's trajectory or improve his or her status as a student, what value does that program have?

124

My concern about Head Start or any similarly situated program is the move to make it mandatory for all three- and four-year-olds. For those who have been nurtured, it could or might be a good experience. What would Horace Mann think of a school nurse giving a lesson plan around brushing your teeth? What is the message a child receives if he has been brushing his teeth since the first one appeared? Will that be the start of boredom? But for those who need it because they have not received good care at home, it will be the start of a catch-up game that is never done.

Is this another inappropriate solution for a misdiagnosis? We must be able to talk about the problem before we can even hope to understand it. Other social/cultural factors negatively affecting education are discussed in other chapters but the questions remain the same. Has the inescapable circle of poverty become unbreakable by education? Elvis Presley sang about "in the ghetto" in 1969 and the beat just goes on and on without improvement but with more children locked into the ghetto of poverty. What would Mann think of all our efforts? Has education eradicated poverty? What will be important for you and your children's needs? Will your school leaders acknowledge differences in children's preparedness or lack thereof? And, if so, they will provide tiered instruction?

"There is nothing more difficult to take in hand, more perilous to conduct, or more uncertain in its success than to take the lead in the introduction of a new order of things."
— The Prince,
Niccolo Machiavelli (1469-1527)

"No idea is so antiquated that it was not once modern. No idea is so modern that it will not someday be antiquated."
— *Ellen Glasgow, Address to the Modern Language Association, 1936*

Chapter Twelve

Palmer Method Handwriting and Other Antiquities

Last year while signing-in at the front desk as a visitor at my local high school, I saw a notice that caught my eye: "Please PRINT all information."

Nothing happens in a vacuum. Shortly after seeing that notice, I saw an article in *The Wall Street Journal* online on 11-3-10 reporting, "the Post Office Can't Read Scribbles ..."

Perhaps you have noticed that I am a reader of the *WSJ*; unfortunately for them, many people think of it as only a business paper. There is, however, excellent writing on so many contemporary events, actions, trends, lifestyle and demographic changes in its pages.

Several other articles have been written recently about the Post Office's Atlanta Mail Recovery Center that address multiple issues, but it was the reference to "scribbles" that caught my eye.

Two years ago when I was doing my outline for this book I knew I wanted to talk about handwriting. I had been observing for about 20 years the deterioration of handwriting. Frequently my reaction was almost knee-jerk. When I was a child, there was a correlation with academic success and handwriting.

I wondered if there were a connection between those mundane Palmer Method writing exercises (rows of repeating overlapping circles or running vertical strokes done within the lines on notebooks) and brain development with eye/hand coordination. I have also wondered if the current younger generations' brains are inadvertently being changed by how they use their hands. For example, think of a young child with a remote unit or cell phone in his hand versus a much older person. Using myself as a model, I admit that with the TV remote I hold it in my left hand and use my right hand digits but not my thumb to punch in the numbers. I have heard so many teachers comment that children's brains are wired differently now. I am pleased that the behaviors are being noted but concerned that we do not know what this means.

And so it begins.

We are in another major transition and, for all intents, it is occurring without much thought. This is called the Information Age, yet the problem is a loss of knowledge.

Will we need a Rosetta stone (the real one, not the language program) in the near future for our great-grandchildren to read old family records? Will the preserved ledgers containing United States' Census data become indecipherable? There is so much available for genealogical searches, such as with Ancestry.com, but you must be able to read cursive handwriting. I admit that I am a romantic yet I am also very practical.

Here is a story of a current chasm of knowledge that is a problem in higher education directly related to handwriting. A young neighbor needed a physics class and her current school would not be offering it again until the next year. My young friend found a summer class at another school at great expense.

On a visit one day, I found my friend at her dining room table studying and fretting. We chatted and I probed a little deeper as to her difficulty with her physics class beyond the fact of the subject matter.

My young friend informed me, to begin with, the teacher was older than me — really old — and his notes were awful. He would give a handout on his outline but my friend could not read the writing. I asked to see his notes.

BINGO! They were in good cursive, not block printing. I could read them but this young person only had one year of cursive in third grade and had not used it otherwise.

This is a serious breakdown in communication but it highlights problems that occur in transitions.

I was taught the Palmer Method of cursive handwriting. There are other programs of cursive in this country and across the world: cursive Arabic, Roman cursive, cursive Greek, English cursive. Cursive simply means the letters are joined together in forming words; from the Latin "cursivus," meaning flowing, to the French "cursif," meaning running. I tell you this because in Australia handwriting is called running writing and in New Zealand, linking writing.

Whatever it is called, wherever, handwriting involves using the hand; therein is part of the current problem. In 2006, only 15% of high school students taking the SATs used cursive writing on the essay questions as reported by *The Washington Post* on 10-11-06.

Where does this leave us?

With all the demands on a teacher's time in the elementary classroom, I understand schools dropping cursive handwriting. Keyboarding skills have become crucial, particularly in pursuing online learning that will become a lifelong event.

However, I have come to wonder if printing block letters will also disappear, because they will not be writing once they learn the alphabet. Most high school students, even here in rural Massachusetts, transmit their homework and other papers electronically.

For many learning disabled people, voice-activated typing programs have enabled them to work academically. Will we be talking about dropping typing also because of voice-activated devices? These changes are occurring faster than institutions are able to absorb.

Will contract law need to change? How will we make a signature? Have we already returned to "X" marks? Do you ever wonder about the signatures on credit card machines where all you have to write is a squiggle? Will handwriting become a learning activity such as the study of Latin or Greek for only a few in our society?

Or can handwriting be an exercise a family might provide at home as part of a brain exercise? There are teaching Web sites available for Palmer Method handwriting exercises.

I do not have any solutions for this issue, I just think leaders in education should be aware of it and families can make their own choices, if they are informed. However, as we learn more about the brain and its development, I am seeing contemporary articles looking backwards for current information. *The Scholastic Parent and Child* magazine in March 2011 included an article, "The Great Write Way," about the benefits of good penmanship and academic achievement. Does your school see this as a concern to be addressed? What do you think about it?

And what about spelling? Who needs that? With spell check, is it becoming obsolete to teach spelling? Have you ever had a paper or a piece of writing where spell check missed your incorrect word that happened to be an incorrect usage but spelled correctly?

Working on several school spelling bees over the years I have noticed that too many kids do not break the word into syllables or even understand that concept.

How many spelling programs has your school had over the last twenty years? Do you have family members who never learned to spell because some expert decided it was no longer important since it is an ability not possessed by everyone? The pendulum has swung back and forth too many times but it is another example of changes made with no accountability although our children can and do suffer the consequences.

Spelling is part of our language but it is occurring in so many different formats. Consider the following words: PHAT, OMG, LOL RU. Now I see the letter "Z" used to denote a plural instead of the traditional "s". Texting, tweeting, IM-ing or writing on any kind of electronic devices has spawned new jargon, spellings and brevity. As with everything in life, there are upsides and downsides to this also.

Is spelling obsolete? Or will this be a subject only taught as an elective? From an educational perspective, I would point out that proficiency on e-devices does not necessarily translate into proficiency in computer skills or language skills necessary for many occupations with good-paying positions. If you think spelling has value, how might your family promote it? Have you considered playing Scrabble with your children or grandchildren? Some side benefits to game playing with children are simple good fun along with subtly teaching strategic thinking.

I think handwriting and spelling were all part of our brain activities as kids. That also included memorization. Somehow doing memory exercises became unpopular along the way. The reality is that some memorization is necessary at the elementary level but also beneficial to brain muscle enhancement. The multiplication tables are only learned by memorization; fortunately that pendulum has swung back somewhat.

Another type of brain exercise we had as children was sentence diagramming. I recently heard a comedienne joking about Catholic School diagramming, but we spoke and wrote correct English. As a visual learner, I can tell you that drawing the line, placing the subject noun, the verb, and the object along with articles and modifiers (adjectives and adverbs) instilled a lifelong love of language for me and conjugating verbs forever changed how I hear language. When I hear students being allowed to speak improperly, I fear for her future successes. "She don't have any . . ." ricochets off my ears, but with the ability to conjugate verbs, a student also is being prepared to learn a foreign language.

	Single Person	Plural Persons
First person	*I love*	*We love*
Second person	*You love*	*You love*
Third person	*He/she/it loves*	*They love*

Think of these elementary exercises as brain gymnastics. Are they a part of your child's elementary school? "It's elementary, dear Watson," certainly applies here.

The difficulty for schools and teachers is that there is no more room in their days, so it becomes a question of handwriting versus keyboarding skills or whatever the local or state administration may be pushing. The constraints on a teacher's time are very real, yet we still have a school day and year that reflect a time when we were an agrarian society. Also we do not have the same length of school day as some of our competitors around the world. We are seeing calls and demands for after-school programs but it is my sense that is driven more by child-care needs than anything else. I think at a minimum we need to redesign the length of the school day — but only if that includes time to play.

I am very aware of the problems with this in terms of re-negotiating teachers' union contracts. With most young teachers also having their own families, I am thinking they might like the flexibility of the day starting earlier or later, but with the same number of hours. We can find solutions about this if we think creatively about time and contracts.

The flipside to the above questions might be, what will you do? Google or Web search brain exercises. Perhaps three minutes of Brain Gym with your children before or after dinner may be to your liking. Spelling should be taught. While some dismiss memorization along with rote work, there are connections between activities and brain development at the elementary level. I have lived long enough to see many things come full circle. When writing, sometimes I still mentally say to myself "*i* before *e* except after *c*, or when sounded like *a* as in *neighbor* and *weigh*." If you had choices, what might you value most? What questions will you have for your child's school?

■■

Probably on a daily basis we hear people lamenting the loss of common sense. But before that became so visible in our society, there was a loss of instinctive, intuitive and inherent human knowledge.

Perfect examples of that occurred on December 26, 2004 regarding the Indonesian tsunami. I heard one radio report only once but with the Internet, one can verify one's memory. It apparently was an anomaly not up to all the horror of the Indonesian tsunami that took over 250,000 lives, so it did not receive more airtime.

USA Today carried an Associated Press report on February 28, 2005 about an island, the Semuele Regency in the Aceh Province of Indonesia, about 150 km. off the west coast of Sumatra. The elders there remembered stories from grandmothers about giant waves called "semong" that can occur after an earthquake. These islanders, so close to the epicenter, had only a brief window of time to escape as the 33-foot waves hit 30 minutes later. But the people listened to their elders. Only seven people died on this island of 75,000 as opposed to more than 90,000 deaths in Banda Aceh. Even the water buffalo knew to leave the beach area and move to higher ground.

Coupled with this folklore, knowledge also was a story of a 10-year-old British girl on vacation with her family. Two weeks before this trip she had a lesson about tsunamis in her geography class. She recognized the sign, the receding waters along the beach, told her parents, and they all fled to higher ground on Phuket Island, Thailand.

The third example was a Scottish biology teacher also on a tour. He recognized the signs at Kamala Bay, north of Phuket, and led a busload of tourists to higher ground.

More than 400 years ago, Sir Francis Bacon wrote "knowledge is power." What kind of power do you want your children to have? What folklore can you share that may improve their lives? I once told a class that old sayings (folklore) may seem trite but they are annoyingly true. "An apple a day, keeps the doctor away" is now officially recognized as part of a healthy diet. How about "A penny saved is a penny earned;" or "save for a rainy day;" "if he's not fishing, he's mending his nets;" "those that lie down with dogs get fleas;" "in a broken nest there are few whole eggs;" "one's name remains above the grave." What stories or sayings do you remember from your grandparents that you might share with your grandchildren? Conversely, how do you feel about others presenting models of behavior to your family members? Perhaps you know of or have observed that legislatures at the state and federal level now write ethics' laws for their own behaviors and that of government employees to fill a void. Do you think this will work?

Roman numerals is another oldie but goodie no longer taught. What will happen when someone refers to section Roman numeral five and it is printed as "V" at a school meeting in a few years and no one can find that section? What do you think? Will this become elite knowledge? Will the engravings on very old buildings be essentially hieroglyphics? Does it matter?

Most legal contracts now use plain language and Arabic numerals but consider how many legal documents exist with Roman numerals.

How will we manage when a meteor storm blows out all communications systems? I think we need to have a good number of people familiar with old-fashioned, basic skill sets. We cannot afford to lose that common sense and knowledge.

> *O tempora! O mores!*
> *(Oh the times! The customs!)*
> *— Marcus Cicero (106-43 B.C.)*

"In the realm of ideas it is better to let the mood sally forth, even if some precious preconceptions suffer a mauling."
— Robert F. Goheen, President, Princeton Commencement Address, The New York Times, June 19, 1966

Chapter Thirteen

Dual Standards and Follow the Money

My grandchild came home from kindergarten with a book she had taken into school to share. Later that day I was surprised to see that the bookbinding had been broken. It was a rather large book, with maybe too much heft for a child to handle. I thought perhaps then it been dropped. I asked her, "Did you drop the book, sweetie?"

I wanted to know what happened, as this child knew how to care for books. She seemed upset. Reluctantly, she told me that someone else threw the book across the room. I asked, "Doesn't your teacher tell the kids how to care for a book?" The quick response was, "Yes, but not for (unnamed child). He can do whatever he wants. He's SPED."

Flashback to Art Linkletter's 1950s TV show, "Kids Say the Darnedest Things" and many may recall what children say is utterly truthful without nuances or filters. How sad at age five a child can see what many adults do not want to see or acknowledge. We have two educational systems for all intents and purposes. When a five-year0old knows that rules apply only to some, it may be time to rethink our assumptions.

SPED – Special Education – has morphed into an uncontrollable system with its own legal protections. I use the word "morph" because this is another example of what happens when original intent of legislation is long forgotten. With the understanding of dyslexia came an energy and enthusiasm to help students with dyslexia to achieve success; after all, was not Albert Einstein also dyslexic? I seriously doubt the law would have received the same level of support if people knew then the potential range of services that would become SPED. Many services are more appropriately called custodial, medical, or healthcare. Many are not directly educational. The various regulations around the SPED laws stipulate almost no cost controls.

This stands in sharp contrast to "regular" education or should I say non-SPED. The naming of and the legal status associated with SPED creates a separation. I suspect if we had had a larger discussion in the late 1970s that included the possibility or probability of between 10-20% of a student population, there would have been changes in the law. In my lifetime, I have come to learn that any and all numbers projected are generally wrong. Government mandated anything drives the costs up.

For us in a rural area, a good example is speech therapists. It is not just a case of supply and demand. Schools must provide the service and pay for it, regardless of cost. When a class of professionals realizes that demand essentially allows them to dictate price, it happens. School nurses, for example, are on the teachers' professional pay schedule because there is no shortage.

Crafting a school budget is also done differently with SPED. Those services are required by law and must be funded. Non-SPED budget items are subject to discussions, revisions, cuts or elimination.

I wonder how people would feel about a cost of $50,000 for one year to transport a kindergarten child outside the district to another school. How would parents feel about paying the salary of a one-on-one aide because a child has behavior problems? And how would parents feel in that situation where, even with an attendant, there are great disruptions during the day? How many disruptions are acceptable in one day? Are three okay but 20 excessive? What is the impact on all children experiencing these outbursts? How would those same people feel if they were parents of a non-SPED child who had limited library, art, or music? How would you feel if your child or grandchild were physically hurt by another student with behavioral or emotional problems? How would you feel if your child's book could be broken even though the student who did it has her own personal aide?

These are some of the reasons why I say we have two classes of students. It seems that privacy laws have come to be a shield. I understand and respect the basic premise of an individual's expectation of respectful treatment in many aspects of life in this era of swirling information. I am talking about laws that keep the public from information needed to make clear decisions. The growth in SPED can be discussed without names; a discussion showing 15% of the school population spending two or more times the amount of regular per pupil school costs might lead to questions. And the extreme end with costs in excess of $100,000 would probably shock most people.

How does this happen? Never underestimate the ability of any group to look after itself; never underestimate the power of any group with legal protections to become institutionalized, greedy, unaccountable, controlling and out of control.

Medicaid or Mass. Health will cover medical costs, but we see schools having to provide the services as parents can choose not to use their own insurance because of yearly caps on services. When laws do not make sense, I have found resourceful people or their paid advocates become creative or "work the system." Do you have a paid advocate working for you? Probably not, if your child is in regular education and not receiving any social services.

The parameters of this debate have been set by those with a vested interest for SPED to continue as-is. It is time to discuss how much of those costs are for medical and health services, out-of-district placements and non-educational expenses. Privacy laws have become a legal obfuscation that bars transparency.

Please note that I have not said to drop services. I am asking that they be called what they are, openly discussed and appropriately budgeted. Transparency on the range of service and costs would be enlightening. We isolate many issues within a budget, such that we do not really know the cost of many governmental services. Additionally, costs may be covered fully or partially by state or federal grants so there are counter-incentives that drive up costs. How many people think state and federal grants are "free" money? Also, if there is a shortage in your area for speech therapists, then new market conditions as determined by regulations prevail; low supply and mandated demand sets the price higher — frequently even higher than experienced teachers.

This unintended consequence has created a division. You see it in the allocation of funds but also in how kids see their world. I have said that we have created two classes of students: one that receives whatever it determines it needs and the rest with any remaining monies.

But there is a division on another field in how kids see themselves. Art Linkletter was right about kids saying the darncdcst things. It is unnerving to see how much they comprehend at a very young age about the application of rules. They then see an unequal treatment. And some SPED kids themselves start to play the system. That a student may need services is not an indication of human intelligence. They know they will not get into trouble and they can actually taunt other kids. The intent was to mainstream but the facts show otherwise. When a young child comments on what she has observed, should we pay attention?

A former superintendent told me that I would get slammed if I tried to even question or point out some of the glaring inequities. That person actually said, "After you testify the next person would be a smiling, red-headed, freckled-faced, pigtailed girl in a wheelchair who would plead for the continuation of SPED."

Again, nowhere have I suggested eliminating SPED. Therein lies the problem. The political arena will crucify anyone who questions or worse yet, challenges, any aspect to this law. The 3Ds get played effectively.

Those who challenge the secrecy of SPED laws are called divisive when challenging certain SPED expenditures after cuts have already been made to the regular education portion of the budget. Who is divisive? Who created two classes of students; one that gets whatever their paid advocates determine and the other, what the budget will bear only? Who moved many expenses from various line items in the state budget and shifted those costs onto the education budget? It is like a shell game so that the public loses sight of the "real" cost of anything.

In my life I have observed that any person, group, organization, institution that cannot or does not account for its activity in the public arena becomes a breeding ground for incompetence, self-serving action, and not unexpected corruption. It is the law of institutions when they are not held accountable that corruption and other problems develop.

One aspect of SPED that is shielded from public discussion is the amount of behavior problems.

How do these come to require special treatment? Do we need to look at out-of- control behaviors that mandate requirements for children to have their own personal one-on-one aide for years on end with no change in those behaviors? It makes a thinking person wonder. Sometimes, as a school committee member, I felt as if I had fallen down Alice's rabbit hole as the Mad Queen, out of control, made her demands.

With HIPAA laws (Health Insurance Portability & Accountability Act that protects patients' privacy), SPED privacy sections and others that guarantee privacy of some groups, we invariably see abuses because we lose oversight. Another concern is the silence in the ranks of teachers who know of these problems.

For full inclusion, one reason generally given is that a child has his/her rights to be in a regular classroom. When is the last time you heard anyone ask about the rights of the other children? How much disruptive behavior affecting your child's education is acceptable? Please note many inclusion programs do work. It is the extreme examples of which I write. It is the blanket refusal to allow fuller discussion that has most families in the dark as to the severity of conditions. Has your child been subject to unreasonable conditions such as these? Do you know of a child physically hurt by a child with an uncontrollable outburst? Does the public have any right to know if a child is making progress as prescribed in his or her IEP (Individual Educational Plan)?

From its inception, first in Massachusetts in 1976 and then followed shortly thereafter by the federal government, we have seen a system grow beyond anyone's imagination. When I say grow, I am including the number of students, actual costs, the range of disabilities, and the types of service. SPED has become a "sacred cow" with no accountability and no potential to be changed unless we demand it. The legal mantle covering SPED has stopped any analysis you might expect to see about any program. But the undermining of respect for law at any level is concerning. Children figure out the walk while we are listening to the talk.

Autism

We had morning and evening newspapers as well as magazines when I was a child in the 1950s. It was in either *Look* or *Life* magazine that I recall an article about autism. I can even see in my mind's eye the black and white full-page photo of a mother with a child in the background. The picture reinforced the content of the accompanying article. Scientists then suggested the cause was a mother's coldness and lack of feelings for her child.

Then it seemed the subject of autism dropped off the popular radar screen. But it is back in full force with Web sites, radio and television public service announcements and many news stories. The numbers as reported on Autismspeaks.org are 1 in 110 children but within that measure, it is 1 in 70 for boys only.

I have seen the heartache and challenges to a family and the child who is autistic but that is not my purpose here nor will I write about the very broad spectrum of disabilities identified as autism as that is a shifting debate. As a grandmother, I have three concerns.

The first deals with the magnitude of the problem. Do we have more children than ever classified as autistic because the problem is worsening **or** do we have better diagnostic tools? Either one is troubling because the sheer numbers should prompt action. However, this debate took an unexpected turn in January 2012 with a Yale Child Study. The DSM (Diagnostic Statistical Manual of Mental Disorders) changes in the diagnoses could cut the numbers in half, reports Dr. F. Volkman. It would be easy to simply say that this is the battle of experts but I contend that it is also a case of follow the money.

Secondly, we need a discussion about funding. It would be helpful if I used a non-educational item as an example.

Readers of a certain age will recall the oil embargo of 1973. For younger readers, I think the most salient way to describe that time is long, long lines at every station or any gas station that had gas. If you need good visuals, Google Images are a great source under "oil embargo 1973." It was a difficult time.

On August 4, 1977, then-President Jimmy Carter signed a law creating the Department of Energy (DOE), the primary reason for which law was to "lessen our dependence on foreign oil."

In 2011, thirty-four years later with a budget of $27 billion dollars with 16,000 federal employees, 100,000 contract employees and funding for more than thirty science labs, where are we? It seems to me that the original mission has been waylaid as the Energy Department has continuously expanded its mission while ignoring the original intent. My point is not necessarily to debate energy so much as to show the lack of accountability coupled then with exponential growth in expenses but no lessening of our independence on foreign oil.

The federal Department of Energy has achieved "sacred cow" status.

Only people of my age will recognize that expression, sacred cow; perhaps to be more current I should call it "Teflon status." No criticisms stick because there is no sunlight on them, no annual evaluation and no accountability because their mission is for the public good and we are to recognize their goodness while ignoring their human component. They assume a life unto themselves as they become institutionalized.

So with autism's popularity as a problem to be fixed, I wonder if we can expect to fall down another rabbit hole. Like Alice in Wonderland, we will see that up is down and down is up. Perhaps it is time to trust but verify.

In another life I taught crime insurance and fidelity bonds. In every class, someone would be offended when we discussed employee theft. Statements such as, "well if she expects me to steal, maybe I should" or "I would never steal" were common. The problem is that a small number of employees will and do steal or pilfer with the justification that "it's only one item out of a hundred" or some other convenient rationalization. Our human nature has good and dark sides. Similar to the constantly changing weather in New England, we rarely have to wait too long before there is a news report about embezzlement, misappropriation, or fraud by some governmental official. It is a known problem in the private sector, where steps are taken to minimize it.

A gift came to me on the morning of January 11, 2012, when listening to National Public Radio (NPR) I heard about "a misspending of $10 million" from the Merrimack Educational Collaborative, a Massachusetts special education group. The MEC is one of many regional groups addressing SPED. This story is as old as dirt. The accused had a salary of $500,000 plus benefits. His business credit card from MEC had charges of $50,000 for gifts for his girlfriend and repairs to a vacation home.

Yes, these are allegations and he is innocent until proven otherwise. Boston.com (the online affiliate of *The Boston Globe*) and others have the story. Towns in the collaborative pay through property taxes for this service in addition to their local schools' SPED budgets funded by local property taxes. I use that word "service" with some reluctance.

Two things in life are guaranteed: that human beings will steal and that sacred cows need oversight. Actually, there is a third. We human beings will also forget about this and go on to create new systems, administrations, new financial instruments, etc. After Enron in October of 2001, there was a push for more legislation. Laws without enforcement and oversight just give us a false impression of someone "doing something."

My final concern is how much interruption is acceptable in a classroom? Again, while there are many advocates for children with physical, mental and emotional disabilities, who will advocate for the other children in a classroom? There can be very disturbing, even violent, behaviors requiring that a child with autism have his or her own one-on-one aide. The rights of one child can and do prevail over the group or class.

Because of privacy laws there is no public reporting of incidents of violence in the classroom, whatever the source of violence, unless it is guns. Teachers today are finding more and more inappropriate, violent behaviors in their classrooms. For some teachers, it is heartache because they are able to see still the child within all the **violence** but they also have a responsibility to provide a safe environment for all students.

Have we have lost our collective sense of balance? Is moderation an unfair practice? Who gains financially from special classifications?

Before anyone rises in self-righteous indignation for questioning this behemoth, allow me to say that this unmonitored system has no boundaries. It also does not have to account for its expenditures. I have been distressed over the years by the refusal of so many administrators to publicly challenge SPED, but there is a quiet, growing frustration behind the scenes with it and some of its extreme misuses.

How much of a school budget do you want to spend on a child who will never work, will always need a personal assistant, and will not be educationally competent? I think I may understand a desire for a child to be surrounded with as much normalcy as possible, but that can cut both ways. How much moaning, crying, piercing wails and thrashing are the other children supposed to tolerate? It takes a lot of energy for anyone to block these disturbances. What will be the "normal" for children when there are so many extremes in their lives?

SPED has morphed from dyslexia to being a full-service system for health and medical care. When annual costs — without transportations costs counted — can exceed $100,000 for services for one year (as services are provided on a 12 month schedule), is it time to remove the obstacles and let the sun shine on this matter?

Otherwise, fetal alcoholism, drugs in utero, infant neglect continue to haunt our children and, ultimately, our schools. NPR reported on 5-1-12 that costs have tripled for the three in 1,000 newborns suffering from drug withdrawal. It is not uncommon to have costs in excess of $1 million at birth. There is a direct correlation with future school costs. With protected status and mandated privacy laws, we have an unaccountable system that does not always help children. Can we expect teachers to be responsible for children who may have brain impairments due to fetal alcoholism?

Lest this strike anyone as extreme, I challenge
readers to go to their own school systems and look
at the actual bills for SPED services. For years, I
reviewed every bill that accompanied any warrant
for payment from our schools. (The child's privacy
was protected by blacking out the name so that no
school committee member could read it.) Is it
unreasonable to expect some results from the broad
range of services? Is it time to let the sun shine on
these protected budgets? If you need pre-approval
for a surgery, how is it any different for reviewing
SPED costs?

More Standards

I have daily reminders of pride in ownership or
good husbandry from our local farmers. Hurricane
Irene caused many fields to be damaged as they
were flooded with sand, silt and other storm debris
from the nearby Deerfield and Cold rivers. It is the
farmers' pride I see as the cleanup continues while
they also continue with their normal chores.

In the spring of 2001, when our school building
renovation project was once again exceeding
approved spending, we were fortunate to have an
offer of space from a local ski resort. That enabled
us to speed the process and save money. I loaded
my truck, as did about 20 others. We made the
move, both ways, at no cost to the school. Back and
forth the volunteers' trucks went efficiently,
energetically and with great enthusiasm.
After Hurricane Irene, unfortunately, we were not
allowed by the school district's legal counsel to
accept volunteer work to clean up the ball fields

150

adjacent to the Deerfield River. That is a major shift in thinking, now seen in many areas of our society. A little tort reform would go a long way to allow volunteers to help their communities.

Do students at your local school have any involvement in the care of their building? Does neatness matter at your local school? Good Enough Never Is! Those words hang over my desk and remind me on a daily basis to do my best. How archaic is that? I hear young people say "good enough" and watch that become an excuse for sloppiness, inaccuracy, and poorly finished work.

I thought about this watching the 2011 royal wedding in London. Even if only 22 million watched in this country (versus the billions around the world), I think it struck a cord with many of us. Compare the "good enough" attitude with all the details impeccably planned and executed for the royal wedding.

I found even the informal education it afforded was amusing and instructive. While some laughed at the hats, a new generation will now perhaps recognize the word "millinery," the making of hats. The many TV shows around the wedding were informative. Watching the handwork by so many talented people was inspiring as various hosts visited the dress and hat shops. Many shows became mini-history lessons, but the attention to detail was rather impressive; for example, grooming the horses by hand.

I suspect all the coverage annoyed many but I suddenly realized the amount of planning and then more planning all led to a flawless production. The thoughtfulness and attention to detail, for me, became a constant reminder of . . .Standards! Do you become annoyed at a public function when the microphone squeals for the first speaker? A preview of equipment can prevent that, if you care about details.

A more extreme opposite example of this might be public sector construction projects. Take any major project in your home state in the last ten years and consider this: How accurate were any original costs estimates? How many delays were encountered? How many major life-threatening events occurred during or after the completion of any project with which you may have some general information? We have seen road projects drag on for years here, yet after Hurricane Irene destroyed the only major east-west road in August, somehow with a 24/7 work schedule and $23 million, restoration work was completed the week before Christmas. The state highway department is to be commended, but it also shows what can be done when there is a will.

I would like to suggest that readers know what their standards are as we go forward; otherwise, someone else will determine standards for your children. Do you value neat work? How do you convey that to your children?

Re-visiting Old Standards
For legislators, citizens and families, I suggest looking back to see how small towns operated efficiently to see what ideas might be resurrected and used again.

152

In my state, for example, sometimes in order to meet the transportation needs of some of special education students we pay the family to provide the transportation and any personal assistant costs that may be required and that person can be a family member. We also will pay the family's additional auto insurance costs, if it does not have the limits of liability insurance required by the school district.

I have no problem with this, as it can actually be more comfortable for the child and less expensive for the school district.

Yet I have been unsuccessful in getting administrators and legislators to see the value of small, rural towns paying a stipend to a family to transport its own children and others. For a frame of reference, think of one elementary child per square mile as opposed to a state like New Jersey that may have a whole school in a square mile. We had precedent for private busing, as it existed until the 1960s. The towns paid individuals to drive students to the nearest high school. Also, the Massachusetts legislature made exceptions from commercial livery laws for car pools during the gas crisis of the 1970s.

My point here is again that we all too often see different standards because we have established "status" for some and not others. Anyone suggesting this type of conflict makes no sen$e generally will be demonized, demagogued or diminished for his efforts.

What is old can be new again. Even one-room schoolhouses in rural areas can have new leases on life with the World Wide Web. While school buses and transportation may seem esoteric, the above example highlights the infrequency of re-evaluating best practices along with an understanding for a legal need for waivers to accommodate life's irregularities. Rules written for a whole state tend to lead to unanticipated problems. It is the nature of the beast. Dealing with human beings can get messy.

Because our rural area has some students riding buses up to 75 minutes per school day one-way, we see many families driving their children to school to avoid the long bus ride, yet we are required to provide a seat for every child. I have ridden the buses, so I can say how sad it is to see a five-year-old get off a bus 75 minutes after she left school. Why can some children have a shorter ride and not others? Are you bothered by the unreasonableness of dual standards?

What standards are important to your family? Does your local school also have similar values or will you find yourself at odds with that school?

"A committee is a group that keeps minutes but loves hours."
— Milton Berle, July 1, 1954

*"Teenagers never fail to amaze me with the
ingenuity of their cruelty."*
*— High school guidance counselor to a student,
Sing You Home by Jodi Picoult, March 2011*

Chapter Fourteen

Bullying

National Review, October 3, 2011, ran a blurb on
New Jersey's new anti-bullying law. It is apparently
very comprehensive. It defines, for the purpose of
implementing this law, bullying as any gesture, any
written, verbal, or physical act . . .that is reasonably
perceived as being motivated . . .by any actual or
perceived characteristic of a person. All schools
must employ an anti-bullying specialist to
investigate and all incidents must be logged in
Trenton, the state capital.

Good grief, for crying out loud, where are the adults
in these school buildings? How did we get to this
point?

Teenagers are very smart. While I doubt that they
could verbalize this, I believe they understand
intuitively and/or instinctively that the Vandals and
Visigoths have mounted the walls and broken down
society's gates. If you wonder about this, take a
moment to watch pedestrians cross in front of your
vehicle when they are about 50-100 feet from a
legitimate crosswalk. Yes, there are jokes saying
"it's all about me," but that is how it begins. With

no consequences for your actions, human beings will revert to their baser natures.

As a child (not teenager), I learned in civics class the challenges any society faces in respecting the rights of individuals versus the larger group. Our young people have been empowered in their bullying by adults who accept this conduct by doing nothing. Because it is a different world now in that teenagers, one step removed from being untamed animals, have a slew of new toys with which to torture some of their peers, including Facebook and other assorted technologies to invade a person's privacy.

A teen recently told me about being "nuggeted." I'm not sure if the word has an official spelling, but a kid knows when it happens because his book bag's contents are dumped all over the floor. All a bully needs is about three seconds to grab the bag and upturn it and then go on her way with all eyes on the mess on the floor. It is a perfectly nasty trick done by cowards. With only minutes between classes this action slows you down and can be embarrassing for girls if they have tampons or other personal items in the bag. The intent is clear: to torture.

I have often thought that the CIA should hire teenagers to develop torture. I am not alone in this observation. Jodie Picoult, a contemporary, well-known fiction author, wrote in *Sing You Home* on page 275, "Teenagers never fail to amaze me with the ingenuity of their cruelty." But in this story also another character, who is gay, on page 229 says "there's something really nice about being with your people." These seemingly two different statements also point out real situations that we pretend do not exist.

Schools that have a "zero" tolerance for guns or any kind of violence do not apply the same standards to bullying in spite of what they say or write in policies. With all the adults in our school buildings, is it really possible that even one adult does not see any of the bullying events?

I think many turn a blind eye for a host of reasons.

From many observations, I see that the aging teacher population is tired on many levels. So little time is actually spent teaching but I think it is time to document time to teaching versus managing behaviors. Would any school administration allow private time management personnel to make an assessment? Does your school allow you access to the building during the day to observe?

Many schools have become custodians of people. Behavior problems are getting worse and so many programs, mandated or not, have not produced intended results. Urban and rural, poor schools share a commonality around the problems of poverty and lower-class behaviors.

The children may have failing grades but they do have knowledge about police, prisons, and parole officers. They are keenly familiar with all of their rights, but not their responsibilities.

A crucial reason for the lack of adult activity, from what I gather in frank discussions with teachers, is a fear of lawsuits from parents of children accused of bullying. With some parents, there is an assumption that a teacher did something wrong first, therefore they presume their child is innocent.

My own children knew if an adult, any adult, said one of them had done something wrong, they knew they were guilty until proven innocent. Now, it is the opposite. This new attitude is a 180-degree shift in our society's thinking. Unfortunately it empowers kids in a very bad way. This has also damaged many teachers' motivations, approaches to teaching and self-worth. Teachers now are guilty of something until proven innocent. Administrators find themselves defending staff against parents. It becomes easier for teachers not to pursue action.

Think about what kids see on TV or in movies. "Mean girls" have been glorified in movies. There have always been mean girls, but in my time, their behavior was not encouraged. It is the psychological bullying that we now know is so very damaging. It has led to suicide in the opinion of a court in Massachusetts where charges have been brought. Watch how mean girls circle around one girl like a pack of wild dogs and then isolate her from others.

Unfortunately bullying has been politicized. I heard a news report that indicated states could be violating federal law if schools do not do something about bullying based on sexual orientation, race or ethnic background.

That is such Political Correctness nonsense! And, it is a perfect example of creating "status" legislation. How is white-on-white or black-on-black bullying to be categorized? Any child's basic instincts, humanity or behavior can be inappropriate if he or she is not taught otherwise.

A school can write a policy indicating that all staff members are mandated reporters but that does not mean they will do it. The New Jersey law seems to me to be putting the responsibility on the child to report an incident of bullying. The spate of new laws and policies are a result of no action being taken by adults, such that kids got the wrong message. If some could get away with bullying with no consequences, why do we wonder at the increase in really inappropriate behaviors?

All the anti-bullying policies are a waste of time. There seems to be an assumption this is a problem only at the middle and high school levels. I know it starts as early as pre-school. Even little ones instinctively react to someone being different until adults create a safe interaction. The "other" is part of our DNA as is aggression, which often serves as a positive safeguard for human beings. Unfortunately, our own aggression is not understood but also the word itself has become demonized such that it only has a negative meaning. Conrad Lorenz' *On Aggression* (1963) was an eye-opener for me in understanding our human nature.

Schools still claim to celebrate diversity but whether it is the nerds, geeks, freaks, drama kids, honor students, whatever — and I do mean whatever — kids will find some reason to single out the "other" for torture *unless* they know bullying will not be tolerated.

However, I must qualify that statement.

Everyday there are students dreading going to
school. As a grandmother, I no longer believe
schools are capable of stopping bullying. When an
assignment is given in a class that will have teams
of two and only one child has no partner, what
thought went into that project by the teacher? Was it
a surprise that an odd-numbered class would create
this oddity? Could it have been avoided? And of
course no one ever sees these problems. But is the
teacher in the room? Is the teacher watching kids
team up? What did the teacher think would happen
with an odd number of kids teaming up in twos?
Doesn't the teacher see one kid trying to get a
partner but being rebuffed by others? What causes
such behaviors? In this case, the kid rebuffed had
received the only "A" on a recent class test. No
other kid wanted to partner with an "A" student.
This had nothing to do with race, ethnicity or sexual
orientation. Isolation in middle and high school is
probably the worst thing that can happen. How hard
is it for a teacher to see a kid being isolated? Or are
they too demoralized by all the mandates, policies,
regulations and deviant behaviors that impede
teaching?

Also what message is sent to students when a
teacher tolerates a bully's inappropriate behavior
directed at her in a classroom? A teacher may think
it is okay with the rationale that "it is not personal"
when it is personal if a student disrespects a teacher.
Or is this the summation of complete "whatever"
thinking after all our rationalizations, justifications,
and /or excuses for bad behaviors?

Family members might consider discussions with children to deal with these situations before they even start school. If you rely totally on the school, your child could be hurt badly, physically or psychologically. It can be quite a shock for a child raised to be polite and well mannered to encounter mean behaviors.

What story will you tell your children to prepare them for the inevitable bullying that they will see or receive at some point in their education or in a neighborhood?

After I finished this chapter, I was reading a mystery novel by Faye Kellerman, *Gun Games,* when I came across **another** new term to describe yet another high school bullying tactic. It is called "crowding." A teen might be walking alone along a school hallway and suddenly there is a dozen kids walking next and around her, such that all look to be part of a crowd; meanwhile the kid in the middle is groped, asked for money, flicked in the back of her head and enduring any other intimidating action the beasts are able to conjure. That, Kellerman felt, this was an important part of the story is a good sign of some adults being more aware. We adults must keep alert.

Early in my tenure as a school committee member I was the lone vote, if memory serves correctly, to oppose a school policy that prohibited self-defense. I was told that it is the responsibility of a child to find an adult and report any problem. I countered that that is hard to do when one is getting the stuffing knocked out of one in a bathroom. I think the above example of "crowding" so sums up not only how vicious bullying is, but also how sneaky kids have become.

In the 1970s my son came home from first grade and told me he had a new friend. But he was upset because the other kids on the school bus were making fun of him, particularly of how he talked. I asked if he wanted to invite him over one day after school. I made all the arrangements. The boy arrived. I forget all the details of how he got to our home. What I do remember distinctly is the child's extraordinary verbal skills and vocabulary at a genius level! So, yes, he talked funny for a six-year-old but the two boys had a love of dinosaurs and mummies. It does not take much for children to see differences that they do not understand, hence they may attack if no one teaches them otherwise at home. For me it is so sad to see bullying actually starting at such a young age, but it does.

"It is our choices . . .that show what we truly are, far more than our abilities."
— J.K. Rowling, Harry Potter and The Chamber of Secrets, 1999

"The most potent weapon in the hands of the oppressor is the mind of the oppressed."
— Steve Biko, anti-apartheid activist, 1946-1977

"When television is good, nothing is better. When it is bad, nothing is worse."
— Recalled on the 25th anniversary of Newton N. Minow's, (Federal Communications Commissioner) "vast wetland" speech, Nightline, ABC TV, May 9, 1986

Chapter Fifteen

Good TV

Imagine for a moment that you are an alien from outer space. You have just arrived in the USA on planet Earth. It is nighttime. There are some street lights, some outside lights, but almost all the houses have blue, sometimes blinking, lights pulsating through the windows. Oh, it is a moving picture box or screen that tells some stories, but what is with all the people talking about toilet paper every six minutes? If not toilet paper, what then is the obsession with an erection? As with any drug advertisement, the best part is listening to the rapidly spoken, potential side effects. This is a great way to laugh with teenagers who love the absurd.

I have made many references to TV in this book for several reasons. Over my adult life I have encountered too many leaders, administrators and directors of public policy, particularly in education, who do not watch TV. They typically are proud of that fact. Perhaps they are cultural snobs? Whatever their reasons, I think they are missing the boat in several ways. I am suggesting a different approach to TV with our highly visual society.

First is the ubiquitous presence of TV — it is everywhere. Did I just teach you a new word? Thank you, but this is how children learn to read (and speak) but also to comprehend the word's meaning in a sentence. Think about the TV show "Jeopardy," as it uses a similar approach having a clue within the answer.

When I say TVs are everywhere, I am including homes from rich to poor. A teacher shared with me a lunchroom conversation of teachers. One of them made the correlation between households, income levels, reading levels and the number of TVs in a home. This teacher had asked her class how many had TVs. She was surprised to find that they all did and each child had one in their bedroom.

That class also had 100% of its students on a free-and reduced-lunch plan. The 100% may be an anomaly, but that is not the point. Why does that matter? Here in western Massachusetts' rural areas TV is only available by satellite services that are very expensive.

TV has become a necessity in the minds of most people. This is a classical case of perception becoming reality. I would prefer if families could distinguish between wants and needs, with needs being prioritized first.

Secondly, just looking at elementary schools from an educational perspective, low-income households generally have the weakest reading scores **and** these children generally lose reading skill levels during each summer. Each September, and possibly into

October or November, teachers are playing catch-up for the summer loss of skills.

Thirdly, something else is happening. Costly private schools are also seeing a lack of reading comprehension. I see this as confirmation of how visual we are becoming. I do not see that changing but, as with anything in life, perhaps some balance is in order.

With TV's tremendous influence, it can be for good or not. My personal preference is for selected TV viewing. We all have the power, if not the self-control, to turn off the TV when there is no appropriate viewing for children. If you or your children do not like quiet or you need some sort of "white noise" in the background, music of any kind can be very satisfying, yet that solution becomes problematic in classrooms.

More than twenty years ago I discovered as a trainer in a corporate training and education setting that students then under the age of thirty would grow visibly restless and even bored. Some, of course, may have been in the wrong field of employment, however, as I thought about it, I realized that this younger group had grown up with "Sesame Street" followed by MTV for music videos. Both had strong entertainment values. I changed up my presentations with lots more interaction. At the end of a class, I left five minutes for an "Insurance Jeopardy" game as another vehicle for transferring information but in an entertaining fashion.

Teachers will tell you that classes have their own personalities. They personally observe the differences year to year. But life-long teachers, the Boomer teachers approaching retirement or recently retired, will also tell you that students today are so very different. Am I just stating the obvious? No. I want to go a step further. If we know students are very different in many ways, what are we doing about that as it relates to teaching? Our students being more and more visual does not translate into their being readers.

In the next chapter I'll discuss reading, but here I want to say to parents and teachers that some TV has a valuable place in education at home. I must add this includes the Internet, however I see both of them becoming one in the relatively near future. It is already possible to buy a TV that is computer-compatible. Also with Web-streaming videos, what is the difference? The *Wall Street Journal's* online edition has videos — live interviews — too. Again, how is this different than TV?

With selective choices in viewing, parents can decide what, how much and when TV or any screen viewing can occur. I fear that with some TV getting to be so trashy there will be a move for government to regulate TV viewing for children. We as families have the power now to make choices, and that choice may include selective TV watching.

For example, there are a couple of TV programs that show how things are made. I happened to take my first senior citizen bus trip last year that included in the day's activities a tour of the Anheuser-Busch Budweiser Plant in Merrimack, NH. For any reader who may have just snickered, remember: we seniors need to be responsible for our own mental and physical activity; the how is up to us.

I thoroughly enjoyed the tour. It was educational, informative and fun. I saw a factory floor that was more than four football fields in size. This was not a Henry Ford-type of factory with assembly lines manned by humans every few feet. It was totally automated with no humans on the factory floor. While overall factory jobs have decreased, overall productivity is up due to technology. Manufacturing jobs in most cases now include a pre-requisite for computer skills.

I think we have separated our children from the world of work. I was distressed when President Clinton said that all children have the right to go to college. Now it was a sound bite, so I don't expect great depth of thought, however, that will not happen for a host of reasons. My preference is to be realistic in goal setting. At this time the majority of young people will not have degrees but they will need jobs, as discussed in chapters six and seven. Also, the currently un/under-employed recent college graduates statistics is scary.

Where will they work? As a parent watching a TV show such as "How Things Are Made," you can expose your child to different kinds of work. The Home and Garden Network's "House Hunters International" shows how small the world has become and how much we all have in common. It is also an example of work skills that have no country boundaries.

The Food and Cooking channels occasionally have hosts cooking with children, their own or guests. If your child cooks with you, you are preparing him or her to take care of herself. And the flip side to that is how proud a child is when he prepares food for his family. Perhaps, long, long ago, we simply referred to this as family chores, but wc did learn some responsibility as a member of a family. It is the same for the larger society. We all have some sort of work to do to make it function. I vaguely remember the 1950-51 TV show "Buck Rogers," which primed my generation's imagination and we were then receptive to President John F. Kennedy's call to put a man on the moon. Ken Burns, with his various documentaries, has put a new spin on old photos as a vehicle for teaching history.

What will be your family's choices about TV? How might you use TV to augment and expand your child's world of knowledge?

"It's not so much that I write well – I just don't write badly very often, and that passes for good on television."
— Andy Rooney, Time magazine, July 11, 1969

*"When they entered the Defence Against the Dark
Arts classroom they found Professor Umbridge
already seated at the teacher's desk, wearing the
fluffy pink cardigan of the night before and the
black velvet bow on top of her head. Harry was
again reminded forcibly of a large fly perched
unwisely on top of an even larger toad."*
— Harry's impression of Delores Umbridge,
Harry Potter and the Order of the Phoenix
by J.K. Rowling, 2003

Chapter Sixteen

Civics

I am so old, I actually remember having civics
classes in grade school, now known as elementary
school. We were taught about this democratic
republic, its creation, the debates around its
formation and its gifts to us. We were also taught
that all of that could be lost if we were not vigilant.

I do know precisely where my love of history and
involvement in civic affairs originated: my parents.
Sometime in 1952, definitely before our August
move from Philadelphia to the growing suburban
town of Willow Grove, I was outside playing with
my siblings on our swing set. The mailman
delivered a huge envelope for my parents from
Washington, D.C. The memory is still so vivid
because I was in awe of my parents receiving this
from our nation's capital. My mother explained that
my dad had written a letter asking for information. I
can see in my mind's eye the booklet on the House

Un-American Activities Committee. Initially my parents and then, in elementary school with letter writing exercises, I learned about the power of the pen along with my responsibilities as a citizen.

The formats have changed over the years. Can anyone doubt the impact of the 450,000 telegrams sent to the White House after the so-called Saturday Night Massacre, the firing of Independent Special Counsel Archibald Cox during the Watergate Investigations? *The Washington Post* reported on October 20, 1973 that Congress received more than a million letters also protesting Cox's firing. Now with the blogosphere, Web sites, Facebook, Twitter, etc., news can and does travel quickly – not all of it accurate, nonetheless, the written or spoken word from citizens still has the power to move, change, stop, initiate action.

Somehow, somewhere along the way in my lifetime we have forgotten the tenuousness of our country in the relative scheme of humanity's existence. The United States of America is still an experiment within the relative scheme of mankind's history.

It is ours to lose.

When elected officials, various media and textbooks refer to our country as a democracy, I wonder how much we have already lost. When a child in your family asks, "Why doesn't the total popular vote count in the presidential elections," what will be your response?

While we were taught in civics classes about our rights, we also taught about our responsibilities as citizens. We have a rights or entitlement society because we no longer teach the other half of the equation of citizenship. Civics is a branch of political science that shows our wonderful rights coupled with certain duties of citizenship.

In 1949, George Orwell wrote *1984* about a fictional totalitarian society. Previously I have referred to political science and science fiction as great learning or teaching tools. Today, I find the numerous, constant PSAs (public service announcements) to be a contemporary version of "newspeak" from *1984*. They are eerily similar.

It is subtle, but within all PSAs, the message we subconsciously see (hear) is the belief that the government is our caretaker with all the information we need to live successfully.

At a large airport after 911, I was horrified to see signs among the multiple warnings saying, "inappropriate humor will not be tolerated." I spoke casually with the guard moving us through the then-new procedure of taking off shoes. I said, "I hope no woman ever puts a bomb in her bra," for which I was told that was not acceptable talk. Who could have anticipated the underwear bomber? Well, maybe people who read science fiction.

The TV ad for the National Flood Insurance Program is a good example of the level of presumed ignorance. Have we become so separated from our natural world that we are surprised that low lands near rivers, for example, tend to flood on an occasional basis – particularly after severe, prolonged, heavy rains in densely developed areas with inadequately-sized storm pipes that can not handle the increased flow of water from impervious surfaces?

In the same vein, is there anyone out there who has purchased a homeowner's or renter's policy that does not have a huge, stick-on message warning that the policy does not cover flooding? Yet, after every major storm with flooding, the media shows people who are angry that their homeowner's policy does not cover it. This sets up another scenario of "unfairness" as defined by the media, not the terms of the policy.

Are you seeing increased messages from various levels of government? Signage for "Amber Alerts" is now being used to remind us here in Massachusetts how easy it is to renew our licenses online— as if we needed more signage on our highways. We are surrounded by so many warnings. Do you find yourself blanking out many of them?

There are radio ads — and that includes online streaming radio — that tell us to lock our desks at work to avoid theft from a fellow employee. NCPC.org (National Crime Prevention Council) is part of the United States Justice Department.

Our schools and towns also have mass telephone systems to send out emergency messages. It is a matter of opinion, though, as to how many of them are really emergencies. A call about a fundraiser would not meet the definition of emergency but our officials cannot resist the urge to "inform" us.

None of this should surprise older readers. Marshall McLuhan's 1964 *Understanding the Media* became the pre-cursor to his 1967 *The Medium Is the Massage,* commonly referred to as *Message.* At this point, there is almost no distinction, if you consider how we are massaged (manipulated) by various messages (ads).

The distinction without a difference, though, contains elements of maneuvering, concealment and even chicanery.

An early example of media impact, influence and insidiousness would be the Nixon-Kennedy presidential debate in 1959. Those who listened to the debate on radio thought Nixon won the debate, however TV viewers overwhelmingly thought Kennedy had won. Viewers still remember two major physical details of that debate: Nixon's five o'clock shadow and Kennedy's golden locks.

In 1950, only 11% of Americans owned TVs; in 1960, 88%, so you can see how politics changed forever. This is a crucial turning point in how we Americans receive much of our information, but from my perspective, the early stages of our becoming a visual society.

Why do I mention this?

The visuals that surround contemporary politics are like "American Idol" without any substance. John Adams (1735-1826), our third President, wrote in *The Boston Gazette* in 1774 about " a government of laws, and not of men," an expression common at the time but not original to Adams. Sometimes our politics seems to be all about appearances, promises to do "something" and stage presence and oratory. Sometimes the law as discussed now seems to have no resemblance to law as written. If we lose respect for the law, we do not have too much more holding us together as a nation.

Learning about civics we learned to be part of a something – our town, schools, state or country. A recent suggestion that public school students have to clean classrooms has created a brouhaha, but a local, private school in my backyard has all students and faculty take turns cleaning, working in the kitchen and doing other chores to keep the school functioning. The students are learning: to be a part of something, that life is messy, and no one is above work.

I have seen classroom floors in public schools with littered papers and wonder "how do we allow children to be so careless, sloppy or irresponsible?"

In the spring of 1772 in Braintree, MA, John Adams said, "There is danger from all men. The only maxim of a free government ought to be trust no man living with power to endanger the public liberty." Separation and enumerated powers were important details in our founding. It is the details about how our government works or doesn't work that are missing now in public discussion or news reports.

Somewhere, someone within the U.S. Postal Service decided to make a change to the series of "Forever" Flag Freedom stamps; now there is a word under the flag. The four words randomly applied are: Freedom, Justice, Liberty and Equality. Hmm . . . .did someone confuse us with the French motto of Liberty, Equality and Fraternity? Or is it only reflective of today's schools teaching fairness as if life can be made to be fair?

When fractions are called equal shares, I despair. When a Generation X, college-educated person asks why the popular vote doesn't elect the President of the United States, I worry. When the crowd makes demands for our democracy, I shudder. The House of Representatives has elections every two years so that it may be responsive to citizens seeking changes, while the Senate's six-year term is to allow tempers to cool and clear thinking to prevail. I suspect if we were to ask some people today, they would want elections every time they disagree with a politician.

Politicians can and do say whatever works for them. They are able to do that because of our current overall ignorance level. Have you ever watched any "man-on-the-street" interviews? The younger the age of the person correlates directly with the probability of an incorrect answer. When you know or believe nothing, you will believe anything. President Obama, when asked about American "exceptionalism," responded that he thought other countries probably thought they were exceptional people too. That response sounded more political than educated. We are not an exceptional people but our form of government is exceptional – not perfect, but capable of being changed without a violent revolution. It is why we still attract legal immigrants from around the world. I would challenge any middle or high school to give their students the same test that new citizens take in the course of becoming citizens. There is a rights-based mentality that exists now. We have not taught the corresponding other half of responsibility of citizenship.

However, the good news is that the fifth Harry Potter movie drove home to all, young and old, what happens when variations of totalitarianism appear. Professor Delores Umbridge, who took great umbrage from the Ministry of Magic, was the epitome of a regulator. All the notices hung on hall walls were restrictive. Students at Hogwarts could see and feel their world constricting. Even so-called benevolent dictators, bureaucrats and others who see their role as protecting us, all limit us.

A very good example of that is the volunteer ambulance service where I live. More than 50 years ago, several town fathers saw a need for an ambulance emergency service to the hospital twenty miles away. Now with the state Executive Office of Emergency Medical Services overseeing all ambulances there is a monthly parade of new or proposed regulations. The 200-250 ambulance calls a year from the four towns served by one ambulance are not enough to warrant a full time, 24/7, service. In my experience, some of those regulations are needless. They also inadvertently make volunteer services almost impossible. How can that be good for our rural area? If your job is to oversee and write regulations, then that is what you do.

I became an EMT to help people, as many people helped my family when my late husband Allan had two heart attacks. That is reality matched by no TV show. One of my earliest experiences as an EMT was an eye-opener. I was taking a patient's pulse and I looked at the interior of her wrist to find a number tattooed there!

While I have shared my perspective on ambulances, I would suggest that school personnel review their regulations. How many are meaningless in that no one ever reads most mandated reports? Are experienced teachers engaging in passive/aggressive behaviors when it comes to silly reports? I suppose it is good for historians that bureaucrats like to keep records, secret as well as open, to document their greatness. A new friend found this to be true when he traveled back to Hungary after the collapse of the old Soviet Union. There he found in KGB files — the orders for his own execution. Happily, he escaped Budapest in the 1956 Hungarian Revolution the day before the city was shut down by the Soviets.

We have lost our common sense. We now write policies and create fodder for future lawsuits. Our young people are unaware of civics and our founding history. Revisionists miss the boat. They see the world as good or evil and so assign those roles. Yet Alexis de Tocqueville in the early 1800s marveled at our love of dissent coupled with our conformity. That we then and now have two parallel but opposing viewpoints is part of our humanity. His comments about the vitality of the town square or marketplace still ring true today. It is our mobility, the ability to move — up or down; educationally, economically, physically — that still draws legal immigrants to this country.

However, I wonder what he would write today if he were to visit. Would he wonder where all the workers have gone? What would he think about a government that wants to know if you had any barter transactions when you file tax returns? Are we really ready to put a value on people exchanging perhaps babysitting services? Would he and Ben Franklin think that we have lost our way?

"The preservation of the sacred fire of liberty, and the destiny of the republican model of government, are justly considered as deeply, perhaps as finally staked, on the experiment entrusted to the hands of the American people."
— George Washington, First Inaugural Address, April 30, 1789

"The basis of our political systems is the right of the people to make and to alter their constitutions of government."
— George Washington, Farewell Address, September 17, 1796

"During times of universal deceit, telling the truth
becomes a revolutionary act."
"Big Brother is watching you."
— George Orwell, pen name of Eric Blair

Chapter Seventeen

Daniel Patrick Moynihan from Vilification to Vindication

You may find this hard to believe, but Internet access is still limited to dial-up for many in this area. As we struggle for access to this modern convenience, there are pockets of service. Fortunately, I have DSL service. The Internet has made and will continue to provide access to information and entertainment.

I have always liked New York radio when I travel to New Jersey. Now I can listen to it on my computer while I am working. I tell you this because an advertisement has caught my attention. The ad tells us:

> " . . .our organization started on the poor, immigrant streets of Brooklyn in 1907. Four courageous women looked into the eyes of the old and sick people in desperate need and deserving kindness – and they did something. They founded the Brooklyn Ladies Hebrew Home for the Aged. With the help of charitable support, the home provided poor, elderly members of the community with quality health care and a

home where they could spend their final days.

And so began the story of MJHS.* Rooted in the values of compassion, respect and dignity for every individual regardless of who they were, where they came from or how much money they had. Those values have guided us every step of the way since then. In a very real sense, we recreate our founding moment every day . . ."

* Metropolitan Jewish Health Services

This radio ad reminded me of another major event also at the turn of the 20th century when Upton Sinclair's *The Jungle* was published in 1906. He detailed through his fiction the story of the workers in the Chicago stockyards. That book is credited with the motivation and passage of the first workers' compensation law in Wisconsin.

But for me, I keenly remember that the "ladies" who came into those Chicago tenements to help families were upper class. They struggled with the lower-class behaviors that they encountered. They felt the behaviors were counter-productive. In many cases, there were also language barriers but, as I read the book, I felt there was no respect for those receiving their help, particularly as enunciated by the original Jewish ladies of the MJHS.

In would be another fifty years before we had an understanding of those differences in behaviors. For me Maslow's *Hierarchy of Needs* so explains our human behaviors in simple, understandable terms. I

used Maslow in Chapter Seven and I refer to it
again as it is the missing type of information when
policy makers (those wanting to do good) design a
new or another programs for those in need.

Self-Actualization
Personal growth and fulfillment
Esteem Needs
Achievement, status
Belongingness
Family, affection, relationships, work groups
Safety Needs
Protection, security, order, law, stability
Biological and Physiological Needs
Basic life supports – air, water, food, shelter,
warmth, sex, sleep

So then and now, for example, if there is an
emphasis on esteem when a child is living in sub-
standard home conditions, there is a break in the
sequence of what and how needs occur and the
order in which they must be met.

With headlines frequently telling us how many
people are in poverty, particularly children, perhaps
we need another type of discussion or at least a
questioning about evaluating contemporary events.

I would like to suggest a current book (2010),
Freedom Is Not Enough by James Paterson (of
academic fame, not the mystery writer). It is
basically a good look at certain social programs
over the last fifty years. As a devotee of Yogi
Berra's "you won't know where you are going,
unless you know where you have been," I am
suggesting (again) that we look back to understand

how we arrived at this point with so many hungry children. NOTE: this statement stands now and before the 2008 Recession.

I have only one caveat/criticism of Patterson's book in that it is written around race issues. As an older, white woman living in a white, rural, poor area, I can tell you the same arguments apply regardless of race.

Patterson recounts in 1965 the late Daniel Patrick Moynihan (NY Senator before Hillary Clinton) as a young man working in Lyndon Baines Johnson's White House. He wrote an infamous memo to the President. He dared to ask if the proposed welfare programs would destroy the black family. At that time, there was a 13% out-of-wedlock birthrate for the black community, referred to as Negroes at that time.

He was severely rebuked, chastised, criticized, and ostracized to say the least by many political groups for **asking a question.** Anyone over the age of 50 knows the law of unintended consequences. LBJ's Great Society was going to eliminate poverty in America, just as Horace Mann expected education to do in the 1840s. Perhaps it was (is) the arrogance of the Baby Boomers, but whatever the goal may have been, did anyone expect or dream that we would see such a growth in poverty among children?

Quickly jumping to 2010, we now see a 70-plus-percent out-of-wedlock birthrate in the black community. Incidentally, for the entire country with no distinctions by race, the out-of-wedlock birthrate is 50%. Yes, I do understand that many, probably 50%, see marriage as irrelevant but I contend there is a correlation with the growth in childhood poverty. You can believe the TV PSA that says "one in four children in America goes to bed hungry."

Within Catholicism's process for sainthood there is a role for the "devil's advocate," who assumes basically a contrarian role when reviewing a potential saint's life. Or, in secular terms, while I was at UMass in the 1970s, I had a class on program development, implementation and evaluation. It is the third component, evaluation, that is frequently overlooked. Without evaluation, program development is wishful thinking. Without evaluation, implementation can be wasteful or unsuccessful. Evaluator or devil's advocate, whatever term you might use, we need to be accountable.

Allow me to frame this in terms of our children. If someone develops a new math curriculum for the elementary levels, it is crucial for family adults to ask how and when it will be implemented AND how and when it will be evaluated. The six +/- years in an elementary school go very quickly. We need to know if the new program is successful. For example only, I would say the evaluation component must spell out the time frames that could be after three or six months. You see, the people who write the programs have their own expectations of what should occur. So the question is whether it is doing as expected. If not, why not? We cannot afford to lose a whole generation in any area as we did in the 1980s on geography. (Chapter Two)

As a child, I was taught in my civics class that the family is the basic unit of society. In the spirit of Moynihan, I question where we are going as a society in this country. I most definitely question the outcomes of many programs. I think there can be no "sacred cows" if we are to brainstorm these issues of poverty because of their direct impact on and with schools. I often think of the parable of "give a man a fish and he eats for a day; teach him to fish and he eats every day."

So here is the quandary that I have observed in our schools that is a good way to highlight the conflicting perspectives within our society. Children were hungry during the Great Depression, so we set up free- and reduced-cost school hot lunches. Then in the late 1980s and early 1990s children were coming to school hungry, so we set up school breakfasts. By 2012, children were not getting evening meals at home, and 50 states have accepted federal grants to implement school dinners.

I am not suggesting that we ignore hungry children.

As with *A Million Drowning Babies* in Chapter Eight, I am suggesting that we have unsuccessful solutions because we did not understand or clearly identify problems. Perhaps, a look at those just above the so-called poverty line who are not eligible for services might reveal resourcefulness that is no longer needed by people getting many assorted services, such as free cell phones, fuel assistance, housing vouchers, clothing and food allowances. I know families who make good choices. They consider subscribing to a TV service, satellite or

cable, as a luxury. They attend to basic needs —
food, clothing, shelter — first. Is it because too
many people can no longer distinguish between
wants or needs? Do you agree with the current
definition of needs? If there is discretionary income,
how is it used? Most families do not have
discretionary income so when gas prices spike, it
hurts their ability to take care of basic needs. The
increase in the use of food pantries verifies real
needs.

Headstart, a program for three and four year olds
under Health and Human Services, not the
Department of Education, is an example of another
program with history now that can be analyzed. Pre-
school programs were meant to level the playing
field before school. It is clearly successful in the
beginning but, unfortunately, the results do not have
staying power. This is also another area where there
is great debate. I suggest that the question at this
point should be around measurable results. How
many high school dropouts in your school system
attended any pre-school program?

I have said to many educators I know "that they
themselves may be part of the problem." To any of
my criticisms of another new social program, their
response is always, "if we don't do it, who will?" I
guess my Moynihan-type question would be what is
the line between parental neglect and abuse of
children?

If we prepare and serve breakfast, lunch and dinner,
why do we see children arriving at school on
Monday hungry? In areas with second and third
generations on public assistance, is it time to re-

evaluate what is being done? Should we consider using old, closed military bases as boot camps to teach families how to function with schedules, job training, preparing family meals? Whoa; I can feel the kick back on that idea. Well, come up with something better.

Poverty is getting to be very expensive and we are further from eliminating it than in 1965. Recall from Chapter Eleven that Justice Sonia Sotomayor grew up in public housing that was very different from what we have today. This is a call to equilibrium. As we assist people there also must be certain expectations of acceptable behaviors.

Let's get real; we do not know how to even talk about poverty, let alone address it. Perhaps examples from history can help us think.

In Deuteronomy 15:11 it is written: "There will always be poor people in the land. I command you to be openhanded toward your brothers and toward the poor and needy in your land." To this I would ask, is it 10%? Could it be as high as 50%? Is this even measurable? I see a growing public sense that something is amiss. I do not believe that any Baby Boomer thought we would ever see such large numbers in poverty as we see now. Is poverty a forever condition where it is possible to be "on the dole" eternally? Skip ahead to the Industrial Era in England. Think about this: "It is a melancholy truth that even great men have their poor relations," in Chapter 28 of Charles Dickens' *Bleak House*. Now let us sail across the Atlantic Ocean to the Plymouth Colony in Massachusetts, 1620.

My children were raised south of Boston in
Marshfield, a town established in 1640. There were
direct descendents of Plymouth Colony living
among us so that colonial history has a slightly
different feeling. I have made references before
about taking advantage of local history and its lore
to capture children's imaginations.

Miss Elizabeth Bradford was a direct relative of the
first Governor, William Bradford. He wrote of those
early experiences and lessons learned. They quickly
realized that a common sharing of food led to those
who did not work. There was not resentment against
helping those who needed it, but young men did not
want to work for other men's children without being
paid something. Governor William Bradford wrote,
"The experience that was had in this common
course and condition, tried sundry years and that
amongst godly and sober men, may well evince the
vanity of that conceit of Plato's and other ancients
applauded by some of later times; **that the taking
away of property and bringing in community
into a commonwealth that would make them
happy and flourishing;** as if they were wiser than
God. **For this community was found to breed
much confusion and discontent and retard much
employment. For the young men, that were most
able and fit for labour and service, did repine
that they should spend their time and strength to
work for other men's wives and children with
out any recompense."**

As with everything in life, the colony also lost its
sense of balance and understanding of what
motivates humans. It was not a case of abandoning
widows or children, the elderly or infirm. Good

works continued, but able bodies were required to work to feed themselves. Poor farms, almshouses and town farms were set up over the next two hundred years to take care of those needing help. Each state had something similar to a board of charities until the early 20th century with the passage of Workers' Compensation laws at the state level to compensate those injured in the course of work. In the 1930s, the federal government set up Social Security, initially called Old Age and Survivor Benefits. The purpose of this quick, fast, dirty history lesson is to prompt thinking and questions. As you ask yourself questions, also remember that being poor in this country is far more comfortable than in many other countries.

Why is this in a book about education? Depending upon the demographics in your area, it probably has a lot to do with your local school. If you and your family are blessed with a middle-class experience it may be difficult to accept the compromises that are made. It is a shock to be told that you are an elitist if you want higher standards, yet that has happened to me and others I know when we find the school does not have the same standards, particularly if we are told the school will assume parental responsibilities. This happens because there are no consequences to parents for not taking care of their children. Somewhere between the heartfelt-concern of teachers to help children and schools provide breakfast, lunch and dinner, there is a point at which we enable parents' at-risk behaviors that hurt children.

Horace Mann, in Chapter Eleven, thought education would eradicate poverty. Could we have anticipated the growth of the Great Society's anti-poverty programs and the ever-increasing number of recipients? I do want a conversation about this. Why? What is the "norm" in your area? If you have a high percentage of free- and reduced-cost lunch numbers you will probably find accompanying social problems with increasing frequency. In Chapter Four I mentioned a second-grader that could discuss the drug trade. These are barometers that should generate more questions and discussions. Are we comfortable accepting a third generation in the same family accepting assistance? Have we inadvertently created a permanent underclass?

This issue of standards is broader than we realize. Nothing, absolutely nothing, prepared me for the day I picked up two of my grandchildren, then ages six and seven, and the conversation in my truck took this turn: "So and so's Dad is in jail," chirped the six-year-old when I asked about their day. I did a quick mental scan of what I knew in local gossip. Nothing registered. I casually asked why was that person in jail? "Oh, he likes to touch girls. They told him to stop; he didn't. The third time, he was sent to jail." And within all her innocence, she moved onto another subject.

I do not care what names people call me nor do I give a fig that my politics are "wrong." I do not want this to be the "normal" in my grandchildren's lives. How far does the common denominator drop before folks are concerned? Art Linkletter, in his wildest imagination, never could have anticipated something like this when he said, "kids say the darnedest things." When Moynihan referred to the dumbing down of deviancy, I wonder if even he could have anticipated a town of 1,350 people with four level two sex offenders and two level three sex offenders as defined in 803 CMR 1:00?

But if adults question what they see or hear from our schools, they are subject to the 3Ds as discussed in Chapter Ten. Where would our society be today if Moynihan's memo were seriously considered, debated and given serious consideration? About fifteen years after Moynihan's original memo, I was in a discussion at work at an old line WASP (White, Anglo-Saxon, Protestant) firm in Boston. The subject was marriage. My boss said, "a man should make a commitment to a woman." How different is that from Beyoncé now singing "Put a Ring on It?" I am excited about that song. Is it an indicator that the pendulum may be swinging back? Will women want, demand or expect a commitment before a child is born? Geraldo Rivera wants a "Who's Your Daddy?" law. I think role modeling, such as Beyoncé's song, will do more to help children than writing more laws.

This will be seen as judgmental by some; so be it. This is an observation that our children need two parents supporting them financially, emotionally, and physically. Ask teachers that you know about many single-parent households and problems that they have. Walter Williams, an economist at George Mason University, contrasted being black and poor in the 1940s and 50s with a simple, clear observation: then it was **unusual** not to have a mother and father in the house; today, in the same projects, it is **rare** to have a mother and father in the same house.

Whatever your individual thoughts on this when you next hear the public service announcement that says "one in four children goes to bed hungry every night" what will be your reaction? What might be your reaction to a parent sending a three year old to school in an obviously soiled diaper? When called by the teacher, the parent said, "you change it, that's your job." Is it time for teachers, their unions, or administrators to publicly discuss how bad life is for too many of our children? This can be done without violating individual privacy. Sometimes I see privacy laws becoming shields that prevent the public from knowing what teachers encounter every day.

The pendulum has swung so far, people are noticing. That is our human condition. Did many dismiss George Will as a Cassandra? (as in Greek mythology, not the open source data management system) In a *New York Post* column (11-29-98) he called public education "a monopoly that chews up children's lives."

Today, public education has become like the welfare state with dismal results for poor children in urban or rural areas. Elvis Presley in 1969 sang about the inescapable circle "In the Ghetto." Nothing has changed except there are now three more generations of a family in poverty. When institutions become hidebound, their only interest is self-preservation. A very clear example of this was last year's protest by Harlem parents against the NAACP for the organization's position against charter schools, as reported ironically by *The Washington Post* on June 2, 2011. Another example of pending change is Juan Rangel. He is the CEO of Chicago's United Neighborhood Organization (in a *WSJ* 9-17-11 article) who asked, "Do we want to be the next victimized minority group in America, or do we want to be the next successful immigrant group?" People are waking up and demanding choices!

"Noise proves nothing. Often a hen who has laid an egg cackles as if she had laid an asteroid."
— Mark Twain, Following the Equator, 1897

"Classic: a book which people praise and don't read."
— Mark Twain, 1897

Chapter Eighteen

GotGotGotGone

As children we were taught to never use the word "got" as it implied ignorance. It was right up there with using the pronoun "she" when the person to whom you were referring was in the same room. It was only acceptable when referring to a cat or the cat's mother.

Then came the "got milk" advertising campaign and the world where we reside changed. It continues to change linguistically almost at an exponential rate.

In the early morning I listen to NPR (National Public Radio) before I begin surfing various sources of news with differing perspectives and formats. For example, I may be reading *The Wall Street Journal* online while also listening to the New York City show of Don Imus in the morning on WABC-radio online via my computer. Why Imus? Those who dispense humor give me a needed, additional perspective on current events and, in many cases, a general sense of what is on people's minds. If Imus is mocking a politician, he is dead man walking.

This particular morning, the NPR weather report was detailing assorted snow storms and their future tracking when the announcer says ". . . and this system will move quick. . ."

Egads! My eyes cross and I am mentally yelling, "lee, lee, it is moving quick-ly!" My ears have always been startled by those kinds of speech errors.

After harrumphing to myself, I wondered perhaps if I am becoming an old fuddy-duddy. But if so, then why are our students tested on English writing and language skills if it does not matter? What word is the "quick" meant to modify? That is the difference between an adverb and an adjective. If the adverb is an anachronism, then let us say so. If nouns can be verbs, what's next? Is this just a normal evolution of a language influenced by our own diversity? Is slang OK? (Or do I mean "okay?")

More importantly, though, is that education is supposed to be a means out of poverty. Incorrect usage of the English language is as if you placed a large "L" for loser on your forehead in so many fields or endeavors. I am not discussing casual conversations with colloquialisms but recognition that speech, in some situations, should meet certain standards. I have heard teachers also speak incorrectly, so maybe that explains why our children's language is not corrected in school. However, that does not make it acceptable, particularly since we test our children on English language proficiency.

Is this just another social anomaly?

194

I did a realty check with a successful businessman I know who telecommutes with a prestigious New York financial firm. I simply asked him if language matters anymore.

His response is important to those who hope and believe education will be a stepping-stone from poverty to prosperity for family members: "They are raising standards in the business world. The bar has not been lowered but actually raised." He added that writing standards exist and that sloppy work is not acceptable since it reflects poorly on the business, firm or partnership itself.

Perhaps this is a problem only in urban and rural areas. From my observations, metropolitan suburban areas appear to have more middle-class attitudes toward language and everything else. I will gingerly suggest that perhaps some teachers themselves could no longer pass English proficiency exams.

I say this not to create a kerfuffle, but to make a point. I recall then-Governor William Weld (1991-97), taking a great deal of political heat for his comments about teachers. He suggested in the 1990s that the teaching field was attracting the lower 25% of students going to college. The dynamics started to change in the late 1960s and 1970s. For example, think of Hillary Rodham going to Yale to study law. Prior to that time, in broad general terms women had limited choices, such as nursing or teaching.

Younger readers may struggle with that but that is the way it was. For example, I interviewed for a management position in early 1965. They humored me, gave me a test, and told me if the war (Vietnam) heated up, I would be at the top of the list to hire based on my score — but only if the war created a shortage of male managers.

Perhaps parents might want to inquire where teachers received their degrees, in what subject area and their class rankings.

So, if the business world has rising standards and schools do not, then education will not be a stepping-stone into the middle class. I struggle with this. How are kids to learn when the larger society does not seem to care about those kinds of speech structures or constrictions? How do we justify hamstringing, hurting, scarring, disabling our kids from pursuing additional opportunities? This is not what Horace Mann anticipated.

Correct language begins at home, but once a child is in school, I think it is incumbent that we all expect (demand, even) that teachers use correct language and assist children in correct usage. What I have seen is the difficulty for some families when the child comes home from school speaking as his classmates do.

The misuse of the third person plural feels like a smack to the side of my head, yet I understand colloquialisms, as common, unconstrained means of conversation. My grandson wants to talk the same way as his friends. Occasionally, I gently remind him that kind of talk is all right when with friends but he needs to know what the correct word is. This can create a subtle message, which hopefully will take root and blossom later.

Perhaps with the technology of "white boards" and the ever increasing visual nature of learning, we might see verbs actually conjugated again or sentences diagrammed with the proper placement of subject/noun, verb, and object along with any modifiers. Another application of conjugating verbs is the direct correlation to learning foreign languages, a requirement now for a high school diploma. Doing such an exercise on a white board will also be helpful for visual learners. I can personally attest to this because as a visual learner I thoroughly enjoyed doing these exercises on a blackboard in fourth grade.

I know I am showing my age but I want adults to be role models. Their own language should be worthy of young scholars. The first time my six-year-old granddaughter used the word "whatever" to me in response to a question, I told her that I thought the word was rude but also that I knew she had a larger vocabulary than that. These are decisions families must make for themselves everyday when considering the impacts of the larger society.

*   *   *   *   *

Recently in a conversation with a private school teacher we were discussing various changes in our American society. Many changes are percolating up with each passing year at accelerated rate. She is seeing fewer and fewer students who are readers in general so that reading Edith Hamilton's *Mythology: Timeless Tales of Gods and Heroes* has become challenging. This is also a comment on our larger society as I see it.

But is reading obsolete? Are we becoming a nation of non-readers in general terms? This is an observation of changes I am seeing in reading levels versus actual readers. Think about what has happened with newspapers and news magazines. They are straddling two different entities, the paper world versus the online world, but still have decreasing readership.

After WWII, the nation's reading level in newspapers went from 12th grade to 9th grade. At the same time, when they lowered the reading level, readership increased dramatically — an actual 45%. For more details on this, research Rudolph Flesch and Robert Gunning on Google.

For another frame of reference, consider these reading levels:

Newspaper	Reading Grade Level
Boston Globe	12
National Enquirer	12
Atlantic Monthly	11
Better Homes and Gardens	11
The New York Times	10
USA Today	10
TV Guide	9
Readers' Digest	9

At first I thought I misread these numbers when I Googled reading levels of newspapers. It refers to reading levels, not subject matter. If you Google readership/circulation numbers, you will see almost an inverse relationship to these numbers listed above as *The Reader's Digest* has the largest.

There is another way to look at this. The following popular authors all write at a seventh-grade reading level:

John Grisham

Tom Clancy

Michael Critchton

Stephen King

Then there are the romance novels written at a fifth-grade level. That segment of publishing comprises more than 30% of all popular fiction.

Why do I mention this? In all the fog of school reports and politics lies disturbing information.

In my experience in my own state with state tests, almost all energy gets directed to high school scores. For all practical purposes, almost all necessary reading skills are acquired in elementary school. Perhaps I should use an age here since there are variations on school configurations. It is my observation in general that reading proficiency occurs by age ten.

Reading levels can and do continue to go higher, but if they are not achieved at that early age, it is almost impossible to change the outcome. This is why I place so much value, energy, attention and focus on reading proficiency before leaving elementary school.

I would also use first grade as an important marker. If a child is not able to decipher the code of our language then, it is imperative that be addressed before anything else. Although I must repeat that a child who has not seen a book before arriving at school will need immediate remedial work.

How does your family's school address reading? How do they measure? Do they initiate remedial work early enough to be meaningful. It must be done before the child feels "stupid."

In earlier chapters I wrote about the family's crucial role in reading, however when schools encounter those children without the necessary family reading, what is done at that point? This is where the rubber meets the road. If any of our schools cannot teach reading in elementary school to a fifth-grade level, they should be closed. The only exception must be for severe learning disabilities. Reading is the foundation; nothing else will matter without it.

Or are we seeing different ways to educate? Are we even ready to consider other possible means of learning?

Think also about the world of animation, movies, YouTube videos. As a grandmother, one of my favorite animated movies is "The Lion King." What a marvelous way to celebrate the concept of family. Additionally, from an educational perspective, I happen to think that the Broadway Musical of "Lion King" was/is a great way to talk about the various skills and potential jobs available in the theater. When I saw the musical, I thought how great this could be for some of our young students to see the artwork, costume design and creation, the puppetry, carpentry, and electrical displays. As I indicated in

200

Chapter Six, I believe we must have a focused connection between school and work.

What does this mean for education? Reading has always been an integral part of learning in our western civilization. Other civilizations and cultures have had an oral tradition to pass along information but that is not our tradition.

Are we now becoming a visual society? I think so. As evidence I would also point to the new MyPlate.gov as opposed to the old Food Pyramid. It is being touted as easier to understand as many found the old pyramid "too complex!" I find the new graphic a little scary in that the only number used is ½. By color-coding the plate of food, the reader can ascertain how much of each food is appropriate to eat. However, this effectively eliminates any need to measure or understand measuring.

As with everything else there are two ways of looking at this: 1) it meets the needs of a people becoming accustomed to quick and fast information; 2) it is another visual presentation that does not require reading for those who are not readers. Are pictures and the so-called universal icons pointing to a future where maybe only a small percentage of our country is readers? Will reading become obsolete, an elite activity or a segmented activity? Or will the various new e-devices attract new and/or more readers?

Reading has always been an integral part of learning but how is that changing?

I noticed that my pre-teenaged granddaughter was reading comics. When I asked about them, she quickly informed me that they are not comics. The Japanese call them graphic novels and she admired the artwork. A surprise and unintended outcome of graphic novels for her was an interest in the Japanese language and country.

I chuckled that our discussion was about semantics only. I remember the *Classics Illustrated*, originally done in the 1940s but used by yours truly for high school English. *Cliff Notes* followed in the early 1960s for those, like me, who did not want to read the assigned books in school. I now see those books as precursors to today's "graphic novels."

In *God Is Not One* by Stephen Prothero, a professor of religion at Boston University, the author points out that the so-called graphic novel is being used also in India to tell stories about good and evil. Deepak Chopra, an author and frequent talk show guest, has created *Ramatayan*, which is described on its back cover as "India's answer to *The Lord of the Rings*." I am seeing a trend here that educators need to consider. Personally, I felt the success of the Harry Potter series was the inherent need within children to know and understand good and evil in the world. But Chopra also sees the need to convey stories about good and evil and he has decided to use a popular format: the graphic novel.

So, if there are stories we want to share with our children or larger audiences, will they be in this newer form, whatever you may call it?

If so, I have no problem with that if it becomes a vehicle for passing along good stories describing some or all of our collective humanity. Again, the question is always what do you want for your family? What stories do you appreciate? What stories tell of your history? What stories do you believe will help shape your children's moral code?

Before you totally dismiss the graphic novel idea, recall the objections to Moynihan's question. Those who want to make contemporary changes generally seem to run into our collective resistance to change. Well, so be it. What do you want to do for your family? Most private schools from seventh grade forward have summer reading lists. Imagine a student not in the top 20% having a reading list based on graphic novels. Imagine that child participating in a group discussion about the mythical good versus evil character in September when class resumes. Will you value that child's understanding of the story? What does your school think is reading comprehension?

Do you ever engage in vicarious activities when it comes to your children? Were you disappointed, confused or even annoyed by Shakespeare? Would you believe there might be a better way? I do not even remember how I learned about Charles and Mary Lamb but I recall their work on Shakespeare was criticized. Their 1807 adaptations of several of Shakespeare's plays made the works accessible for children. This offended purists.

As a pragmatic person, I found that book to be an effective tool to introduce Shakespeare to children. My daughter, the teacher, loved Shakespeare in high school because her introduction in elementary school was by way of the Lambs' book. With her own youthful love of Shakespeare, she has read Lamb's "MacBeth" to her students so the kids had the gist of the story. Then she used Macbeth as an after school project. The kids "got it." They intuitively understood the play with some help from their teacher. They ultimately performed a successful adaptation of the play for the whole school. Do you believe that kids can do more than is generally expected?

A contemporary example of a graphic book is *Persepolis, The Story of a Childhood* by Marjane Satrapi (2003). Her book is a memoir about growing up in Iran during the Islamic Revolution. A good teacher could elicit a real contemporary conversation with students around this book. This could also be an effective way to introduce the Iranian Cultural Revolution as seen through the eyes of a child. The young teenager challenges her mother about not caring . . .when the mother replies, "our country has always known war and martyrs, so, like my father said: when a big wave comes, lower your head and let it pass." The daughter thinks "how Persian, the philosophy of resignation." These are human stories that a reading level of sixth or seventh grade can understand and feel some kinship with about generational differences.

If we want comprehension of ideas, perhaps we need to consider these types of books differently.

In the 1960s, Marshall McLuhan's *The Medium is the Message* laid the groundwork to be thinking of all the possibilities coming at us. Well, they are here and still expanding, changing, and affecting all. Could any of us imagined thirty or forty years ago the significance of the Social Security Administration announcing that all social security checks will go to direct deposit except for those over the age of 90? We are going paperless!

In the 6-8-11 *WSJ* an article reinforced, for me, how visual we are becoming. In "Don't Come Back, Hospitals Say," the article tells us about "virtual nurses." Patients for assorted reasons, valid or otherwise, do not always follow written discharge orders resulting in re-admission to hospitals.

The virtual nurse, an animated character on a computer screen, developed by Boston University Medical Center, reviews all discharge orders with patients. With this computer nurse, a.k.a. Louise, there is no time limit and the patient can have her repeat any instructions. This becomes a visual and auditory lesson in home care before the patient leaves the hospital.

Another example of visuals versus the printed word can be found in military situations. The business world has for years employed the use of pictorial brochures for teaching employees. Now with Kwikpoint, a registered trademark company, the military has visual language translators. While pointing to pictures, our servicemen can communicate in Afghanistan and many other locations. While Kwikpoint makes the military brochures, they also print many for the medical, hospitality and other industries operating around the world. Additionally in the world of "apps" the military is using apps with more pictures or icons because it is faster for the user. Users are not my age but our young military man and women in the theaters of war or other unfamiliar areas. They need fast communication. These are just examples for the reader to think through the consequences of visual learning and re-defined reading.

Another example from outside the education field is the Channing Bete Company in South Deerfield, MA. They have been producing publications created on market-based research for more than 50 years. Their brochures are reliable resources in various formats for readers of all ages and levels and cultural backgrounds. A major example of their work that has received a lot of recognition is their American Heart Association CPR training material.

It is the amount of drawing or visuals in these products that led me to see how reading is declining — or is it a matter of less literacy?

PBS' Frontline's "Digital Nation – Life on the Virtual Frontier" (2-2-10 and subsequent reruns) has an interview with a college professor who says he cannot assign books longer than 200 pages and expect them to be read. Meanwhile, in the next frame, there is a student telling us how he uses SparkNotes.com to read a quick synopsis of any reading.

It is interesting to in the difference in perspectives. In my own family my granddaughter tut-tut-ed me for admitting I hadn't read Tolstoy's *War and Peace*. I commented that I'd read the *Cliff Notes*, to her horror. She insisted I would then miss the beauty of his writing.

206

Ah-ha, a light bulb moment! I enjoyed some Tolstoy short stories but I did not care for his writing. So why do people read? We expect students to love the beauty of the language when maybe we should be concentrating on the essence of the story. How do you feel about this? It may be important to understand our own motivations so we do not inadvertently turn off a child from reading.

Throughout this book I have purposely included references from the commercial marketplace. As I discovered good software for my granddaughter, I recommended it to our local school. The first example was a "Blue's Clues" CD that absolutely delighted my three-year-old grandchild. She particularly enjoyed the segments that taught matching shapes, patterns, and sets.

Sometimes it takes a while for the dawn to break over this Marblehead but eventually I realized that the school was not interested in anything from the commercial marketplace for educational items. Yet the commercial marketplace is generally years ahead of the "approved" educational concerns.

So as we as a society become more and more visual, what is the future of reading and writing? I do not anticipate reading going the way of Latin in the immediate future. I do see it as a dividing line, for now, that may correlate with an ability to earn a better income. But the future may lie with those who can think, create, or organize based on different learning and teaching methods. The recent news reports about Eastman Kodak and Apple dramatically reveal not only contrasts, but also what happens to institutions that do not change when necessary. Kodak has filed for bankruptcy while Apple is set to produce digital textbooks.

What media might you choose to use with your family for them to learn stories?

If you had choices, what might you value most? What questions will you have for your child's school? The flip side to the above questions might be, what will you do? Google "brain exercises." Perhaps three minutes of Brain Gym with your children before or after dinner may be to your liking.

The pendulum will continue to swing back and forth, as it always does, but if it is another example of changes made with no accountability, our children can and will suffer the consequences.

Whether you read, listen or watch any medium, consider how the words are used. Words matter, whether they are used incorrectly, deliberately omitted, or selectively edited, they ultimately affect your understanding of your world. For example, if you do not remember or know about NBC's "Dateline" TV show that rigged exploding gas tanks on its 2-22-93 presentation, then Google it. Any medium can manipulate us. Everything and more that Marshall McLuhan and Quentin Fiore told us is magnified exponentially in our new digital and virtual worlds.

In 1969, Hillary Rodham spoke to her graduating class at Wellesley College, saying, " . . .Words have a funny way of trapping our minds on the way to

our tongues . . .even in this multi-media age . . ."
Today I have a different sense of that. Now I think
that by the choice of words, our minds can be
programmed to be receptive to the actual content.

Orwell warned us about many things in *Animal
Farm,* but with the character Squealer he shows us
how any person or group can use words to change
language to keep us in line. Think of **any**
presidential press secretary answering reporters'
questions. Watch that person mentally choosing
each word for its 15-second sound bite effect. For
some people, the most news they may receive on a
daily basis is the three minutes at the top of the hour
on their car radios coming or going to work.

The good news is that words can also be
inspirational. Jennifer Hudson visually coupled her
words with showing before and after pictures of
herself that "you can do it – believe" ad for Weight
Watchers. Sometimes, we can be manipulated for
good reasons. I just like to recognize when that is
happening.

Words and stories are not new. While some might
consider reality TV a contemporary distraction or
problem, depending your perspective, the concept is
not new. Think of bread and circuses for the masses
during Ancient Rome. The current book and movie
Hunger Games is just another variation of mass
entertainment meant to keep us distracted. But
Hunger Games — book, movie or comic book —
can be a starting point for discussion. What do you
think about a society that has teenagers fight to the
death?

It happens in all aspects of our lives now. Politics has always been a blood sport, but former President Bill Clinton introduced another element when he played the sax on "The Tonight Show." Now nothing and no one is sacred or special. Frank DeFord commented on Labor Day 2011 on NPR about Aretha Franklin being "the opening act" before the President's speech in Chicago. An opening act, like in a circus or media event; good grief! Is nothing special, sacred or secure from "American Idol" thinking?

"When I use a word," Humpty Dumpty said in a rather scornful tone, "it means just what I choose it to mean neither more or less."
— Through the Looking Glass by Lewis Carroll, 1872

"Books consist of words and ideas, not paper and ink."
— Cushing Academy Headmaster, James Tracy, Class of 1984, UMass/Boston, Fall/Winter 2010-2011 Alumni News

"Work 'em hard, play 'em hard, feed 'em up to the
nines and send 'em to bed so tired that they are
asleep before their heads are on the pillow."
— Frank L. Boyden, Headmaster,
Deerfield Academy,
January 1954

Chapter Nineteen

Childhood Obesity and Wall-E

Are we unconsciously creating an alien race within
our midst?

Think of the 2008 Disney/Pixar movie "Wall-E."
The DVD jacket describes it as a new, cosmic
comedy adventure. The setting is hundreds of years
in the future. More than a cosmic comedy, I see this
as science fiction and that has always been a source
of entertainment, edification and enlightenment.
With it we can allow our imaginations to roam.
Additionally, writers have used this format to make
a point, teach us, and expand our senses.

The scene where the current captain of the space
ship reviews all the portraits of previous captains
lined along a curved wall is really an eye-opener.
With these pictures, you can quickly see the
progression of physical changes. The first captain
was slim and trim. Each subsequent captain appears
slightly heavier than his predecessor until we see
the current captain in a whole new perspective. He
is extremely overweight. He is so heavy that he
does not even walk. But he has no need to walk, as

211

all inhabitants of the space ship move about on their own portable, moveable, multi-purpose, transport chair that function as appendages to their bodies.

When I suggest that we are creating an alien race within our midst, I generally receive weird or hostile looks. Yet, with childhood obesity at an all-time high, is it not obvious that something is amiss? Previous chapters dealt with how children's brains are functioning differently than adult brains as well as how they use their fingers. In our own lifetime, we are witnesses to major psychological and physiologically changes we would not have thought possible 50 years ago. Physical education teachers (formerly known as gym teachers), over the age of 40 know some of the physical changes they are seeing in our children. Everyday they see the children's shrinking abilities to perform exercises of almost any sort. In general terms they see kids needing more breaks. They have limited stamina. We are also seeing girls at a younger and younger age beginning menses. Menstruation and other puberty changes are appearing in second graders.

Part of that is that kids do not "play" outside of their homes or schools unsupervised anymore. I say, "part," as I believe there are other factors, including diet, hormone and chemical additives and possibly unidentified factors in this equation as well. There are many parts and developments to all of this.

In this chapter, I am looking at the lack or absence of physical activity. Kids are taught about inside and outside voices but even outside, limitations seem to be placed on their natural enthusiasm to run, leap, and, yes, yell. Sometimes it seems that yelling, boisterousness and general physicality is discouraged needlessly. These so-called aggressive behaviors may be frowned upon in some areas. At the elementary level, I have felt for a long time that boys are not allowed to be boys.

And, yes, I do believe that boys and girls are different.

So it appears that we keep restricting and limiting even their physical opportunities to play outside at school recess to run off excess energy. Then at home, for assorted reasons, kids are not playing outside unsupervised either. Here in our rural area we do not have drive-by shootings as seen in some urban areas. A side loss to this loss of physical play is we are seeing a lack of imagination in kids. With no opportunity to plan for and organize themselves or to be creative, they are missing one of life's early educational experiences. While there is a place for organized sports, there is the playground of life — a pick-up game of basketball, for example.

Kids used to build their own tree houses; sometimes, their dads would help. Now if tree houses are built, they tend to be mini Taj Mahals. I am happy for the kids whose dads help out, but I do wish we could allow kids some freedom to play, explore, and imagine unsupervised. My children's father had grave concerns about our kids climbing trees. He thought they could fall and maybe break a bone; I felt differently. Let them climb — and know that sometimes means they might fall.

Another perspective on this issue of play and the development of imagination is our country's crucial need to continue innovating. Harvard's Tony Wagner is the Innovation Education Fellow at the Technology & Entrepreneurship Center. He wrote in *The Wall Street Journal*, "Educating the Next Steve Jobs" (April 14, 2012) about the three P's – play, passion, and purpose. Lest you get the impression that this is complicated, think of your own childhood adventures.

My grandchildren play outside even in the winter. After a major snowstorm, the kids went outside, dressed warmly, and began building a snow fort. My daughter sent out a box of food coloring so they could decorate the ice and watch how the food coloring dripped and froze. A local reporter stopped to take their picture because, she said, "it is so unusual to see kids playing outside in the winter." What happened to sledding all day until you were exhausted from climbing back up the hill so many times? That is not a rhetorical question, unfortunately. Snowmobiles here have eliminated the climb back up the hill.

We are fortunate to live with a local ski resort next to our village center. All our school children take a winter enrichment program that includes downhill skiing at a reduced cost. The owner also offers ski passes as incentives during school sales. Children are able to start skiing at age four. Outside of the school program, skiing can get a little expensive, but there is also cross-country skiing, snowshoeing and winter hiking. The point is to get outside, dress warmly and do something outside. Our children are becoming separated from the natural world.

My daughter and her friends take turns with all the kids. One dad called when it was his turn to ask for some help. My daughter arrived to find the small group of kids playing video games. She said, "Look outside." They saw the front field full of lightning bugs. She had them grab their nets and some jars and off they went. My daughter said, "the trees looked like decorated Christmas trees with more bug lights than she had ever seen." But the best part of that whole experience was nine-year-old Sam's comment: "I'm going to remember this forever." Play is not complicated, but play can be full of wonder.

As I was writing this book, I heard an announcement on December 13, 2010 about President Obama signing a new healthy school lunch program as part of the Child Nutrition Re-Authorization Act, which is the same as the Healthy, Hunger-Free Kids' Act. I heard on NPR that "healthy and hungry-free will go a long way to eliminate childhood obesity and hunger." The city of Chicago has taken that even further. *The Chicago Tribune,* on April 11, 2011, reported that home lunches are officially banned in Chicago schools. The reasoning is to control what students are eating.

Who can be opposed to that?

Well, I am. It should go without saying that I do not want any child to be hungry, but within the parameters of political debate, I feel it is necessary to say that first.

Secondly, my problem is how the problem is diagnosed, then how the resulting information is used. In this case, joining these two issues of hunger and healthy seems to obfuscate rather than enlighten the population. As I said in Chapter 19, words do matter. Bagged school lunches are mandated here in Massachusetts on school half-days. They are given to children to take home. Has anyone checked to see if the kids eat them?

I do not doubt for a minute that there are hungry children, but will school breakfast, lunch and dinner really change the neglect aspect and/or the looming obesity? By linking these two problems, we are making a big mistake. What is the cause of hungry children? Without the answer to this, any response to hunger will be inadequate. Obesity is a separate problem, more readily addressed by education.

Both hunger and obesity are examples of additions to our educational systems to correct problems incorrectly identified. But this chapter is about obesity. In "Wall-E" it was clearly a sedentary lifestyle along with the ever-presence slurpy drink in the cup holder of kids' movable chairs. I am comfortable with a blanket statement that too many of our nation's children are sedentary with TV or other electronic digital devices.

Further, I would like an enterprising educational administrator to make a random check of children on free- and reduced-cost lunch program participants. See how many have TVs in their homes and even in heir own bedrooms. If anyone has a right to TV, how do we reconcile that with these same children losing reading abilities every summer while away from school? **If** we decide reading does matter, what would you do about that?

216

How much time is wasted every autumn to bring the class back to the same level they may have achieved in June of the previous school year? Should parents be responsible for the summer decrease in reading skills?

In Chapter One, I wrote about 50% of kindergarten children needing remedial PE. Lest one think I am highlighting isolated situations, I suggest we pay attention to a report from our U.S. Army. NPR reported in December 2010 that Army recruits cannot execute simple shoulder rolls in basic training. The Army acknowledged modifying certain beginning exercises to avoid injuries in the early stages of training.

There are signs everywhere if we only look.

Stand outside a convenience store for a couple of hours, say 2:30-5:30 p.m., and simply observe what is being purchased, at greatly inflated costs. Mostly it will be artificially flavored and chemically enhanced snacks, chips and drinks that can become addictive. This is not a rant against all fun food. I would just rather people make conscious decisions. I do still want, once a year, to go to a country fair and eat fried dough and indulge, occasionally and consciously, in comfort food.

I am not, nor do I want, to be a food police officer. In my life-long observations and personal experiences, I have found that addictions are really hard to kick. I relate that to a child being introduced to an array of chemicals at an early age. It becomes very difficult to get those children excited about a beautiful, red, crunchy apple. Food habits — habit being the key word — can be changed, but only with concentrated effort and hardly with a 100% success rate. For schools to think that they can break the cycle of poor food choices once a child starts school is to ignore what we know about habits, conditioning, and the overall-human condition.

It is a matter of balance and moderation, but then, so is life. Obesity is not just food but also activity. What are the policies of your local school concerning physical education, outside playtime recess, and transportation to school? Generation X parents face a different world than we did raising our kids, such as registered sex offenders. But with no walking, even to a bus stop, are we contributing to the problem? If your school bus policies do not require some walking sufficient or to your approval, what will you do as a family? There is nothing that precludes your family from walking together after dinner.

Visit any mall, sit for fifteen minutes, and observe for yourself how many overweight people you see. We see it all the time but it has been gradual and only now, at the obvious change, do we react. MacDonald's in my area has paper placemats with nutrition facts listed on the back. If you have not seen this, look for it; it may give you pause to think as you make choices. The news is that they now offer some healthy choices.

The NIH (National Institutes for Health) Report, "Physiological and Health Implications of a Sedentary Lifestyle," December 2010, indicates that inactivity is as dangerous as smoking. The various

Wii exercise programs are a good addition to anyone's electronic game collection, but there also inexpensive videos and other applications that a family can use.

Here at my little elementary school a new principal has volunteered her time to lead a before-school exercise program with our students. We have tried this before with a jump-rope program. It was interesting to hear teachers' comments as they found that the kids participating in the jump rope program did much better with their schoolwork. A problem is that these types of programs tend to be volunteer-led.

It might be time to change the structure of the school day and teachers' contracts. For example, a teacher's contract could require X number of hours per day, as opposed to starting and end times being the same for all staff. But those issues are not part of this book.

My sister Rosemarie likes to say, "it is what it is." That being so, while we wait for 21st-century educational systems, as families you might want to consider your own solutions to avoid or reduce obesity in your children. It can start with something as simple as a new mother walking a baby in a stroller —good for the mother's overall health, but also it introduces the child to outside air. We have a basic need for physical activity. How will your family plan for this?

"Imagination is more important than knowledge. For knowledge is limited to all we now

know and understand, while imagination embraces
the entire world, and all there ever will be to know
and understand."
      — Albert Einstein (1879-1955)

"Character consists of what you do on the third and fourth tries."
— James A. Michener in Chesapeake, 1978

Chapter Twenty

Thorns and Roses

I have always tried to find common ground with people. My preferable way is through and with food, as you may have observed. Food is a means to bring people together when sitting around a table. Conversation then follows.

After a very contentious school committee meeting in the 1990s, a teacher suggested to me that committee members needed a retreat to learn how to talk with one another. At our next committee meeting, I suggested a potluck dinner at my home to break bread together and kick around ideas.

A member asked if my home were handicapped-accessible, as the public — anyone — would need to be allowed to join us so we did not violate the state open meeting law! Are you laughing? Yes, it was so silly. It does seem to be an inappropriate response but unfortunately, the individual truly meant it. When public officials have no way to talk across the aisle, is it any wonder that our discourse is so uncivil? And then somewhere along the way we tend to think our perspective is the only true and right way.

So how shall we begin to address this?

Even though I disagree with President Obama in many areas, I do admire how Michelle and Barack Obama seem to be raising their daughters. I heard from my own daughter, the teacher, that her family has initiated the "thorns and roses" idea that the Obama's use also at her dinner table each night after she read about the Obama's doing that. It involves relating something good and bad that happened that day. Each person defines his or her own thorns and roses for the day. The child gets to say what or who made him happy, smile or feel good as well as to acknowledge something did not sit right.

I used to do something similar with my granddaughter when I picked her up from school. I would ask, "How was your day?" Then I started getting one-word answers from her. Initially I suggested that I knew she had a larger vocabulary than a one-word response. This made her laugh. When I received a response of "bad" to "how was your day?" I then said, "What made it bad?" and followed up with "tell me something good that happened."

Wherever or whenever this occurs, after school or at a dinner table, it can be an opportunity to discuss a negative in terms of how to handle it, deal with it, even accept it as well as for a child to hear her own words. Have you ever kvetched to a dear friend and suddenly heard your own whiny words? Sounding boards are just as helpful for children. Even Dr. Suess, in *All the Places You Will Go,* addresses the upsides and downsides to life. Is he negative? Of course not! Consider the definition of criticism: "N.

the art of passing judgment on the merits of anything." Do you read book reviews? Do you listen or read movie critics' reviews? If so, can we find a way to allow a fuller discussion on various perspectives? I suspect not at this point, as our country is experiencing major differences. When those differences become reflected into education, it becomes personal for families with different concerns or positions.

At some point, we all realize that this diverse country has many different perspectives and opinions but also certain commonalities. All parties are interested in an educated populace; we just do not agree how to do it. Do you still think there is only one way?

I am distressed by the "fairness" arguments made on a regular basis in too many elements of our American life. I call it the pre-school position on life that is manifesting itself after almost 30 years of pre-school in various configurations in most states. When I hear that young, recent college graduates are angry because they can't find work and are carrying crushing debt from college, I wonder that with the now near mantra that every child is a winner, gets a trophy, and is praised to high heaven, is it any wonder that there is a great sense of entitlement? Life is not fair. The shock and reality of that is evident on the faces of many young people stepping into the real world from academia now.

Because we are not prepared to hear differing opinions, we can and do make mistakes. I often think of the old Yankee that stood up at a town meeting in 1972 to speak against accepting federal revenue-sharing dollars. For those not familiar with the New England town meeting concept, let me explain.

First, you must be a registered voter to speak, although a meeting may, by vote, allow non-voters to do so. Non-registered voters may attend, but must sit in a designated section of the meeting room. Even the school superintendent, who will present the proposed school budget to each town in his district, at least in my rural area, needs voter approval to speak to his budget. The annual town meeting is where budgets are modified or approved, various bylaws are presented for approval or not, and other town business is conducted. The meeting in any town may have its own small quirks, but any registered voter may speak on any article of business. By law, our town voters consider a warrant article each year at the beginning of business to authorize selectmen, the chief elected officials here, to accept state, federal monies, any grants, or gifts.

Revenue sharing was the beginning of blurring the lines between levels of government and what anything costs. But in very simple terms the old-timer said, "If you accept this money, they will have control over you because you will get used to the services even when the money stops." A common expression in my youth was "he who has the gold, rules."

I was re-reading a 1982 book in which Richard Reeves in *American Journey* revisited the places Alexis de Tocqueville wrote about in *Democracy in America* in 1831. To see Ed Koch, then-mayor of

224

New York City, railing, "we keep getting these mandates from Washington without providing the money," shows how quickly federal money and policy changed our nation in ten years. A month after the dinner with Koch, Reeves recounted a conversation with Jerry Brown, governor of California, who was also in the midst of an unsuccessful run for President. Reeves described Brown as an inconsistent man, both unpredictable and thoughtful. Brown told Reeves "as free citizens, we are increasingly dependent on distant bureaucracies that give us permission to think . . ."

How many thoughtful people do you know who are consistent? People are also like roses with thorns. More often than I care for these past twenty years, I am hearing exhortations at town meeting "to do the right thing" when voting. Only by agreeing to a school budget, for example, are you able to say, "You've done the right thing?" When the parameters of a debate are expressed this way, you cannot have full discussion. What about the thorns hiding within any issue?

As we all ponder what the future will hold, there is one word I do not hear anymore: sacrifice. Within the Catholic culture, this is the concept of willingly giving up something in exchange for a greater good. Within a family, for example, there might be a decision to forgo spending money on movie rentals to save that money for an important purchase. Or this could involve using a public library more instead of buying books. A family discussing, then making a decision to strive for a goal, has unintended consequences. A family then is demonstrating decision-making, choices, goal setting and the ability to set aside a need for instant gratification.

These types of discussions are invaluable life lessons that, as adults, you can share with your children. Each person decides what is a thorn or a rose. In life, we human beings have the capacity for good and evil. It is a heart ache for a parent when your child first encounters a mean person. With movies even glorifying "mean girls," is it any wonder we are seeing so much bullying, as previously discussed in Chapter Fourteen? But sitting at the table or otherwise engaged with your family, you can help your child navigate through this world. You can discuss strategies. Mostly, though, you are enabling your child to be aware, be responsible for her own actions, and to learn to make decisions – all within the course of a conversation. How do you determine your family's priorities? Is it an opportunity to include your children at an appropriate level?

Does your school give the younger children copies of *Scholastic News*? That can be a great conversation starter. The material is age-appropriate and interesting. My family had fun with an edition dedicated to the 100th anniversary of the Titanic. For us, the number of passengers almost matches our town population. For those living in a city, how does the length of the ship at 883 feet compare with the length of your block?

If not at the dinner table, where does your family find time to share, talk, plan, or simply be a family? Is there room at your table to occasionally include another child who might need a little TLC?

However you may describe your world –
community, association, tribe, class, affiliation,
membership, ethnicity, high-rise apartment
building, town – it is time to think about the future
of our children in our multi-cultural society.

The "it takes a village" metaphor can be viewed in a
slightly different manner. In 1969, The Prince
Spaghetti Company made a TV commercial in the
North End of Boston. The North End has been
gentrified since the time the ad was first shot. The
North End was an Italian-American, working class
neighborhood. The ad sought to convince
consumers that Wednesday should be "Prince
Spaghetti Night." An Italian mother yelled out of a
window for her son, "AN-TOOOO-NEEE!" to
come home for dinner. Fortunately, the ad lives on
via YouTube today, if you want to see it. But
missing from the ad was an important element of
that community. The Italian grandmothers, who all
knew every kid, could reprimand them if necessary,
as that was an adult prerogative, and they kept their
fingers on the pulse of their neighborhood. Nothing
was complicated, organized, or directed from some
bureaucracy.

Well, here in Charlemont, "the land that time
forgot," said a Boston TV station in the early 1990s,
we have our own Yankee version of that Italian
grandmother. At A.L. Avery's General Store, at the
meat counter is Paula. Our Paula knows all the
children, gets them to talk or giggle and is our
character looking after the kids. Do you have such
an adult in your kids' lives? Who are the immediate,
second-tier and further-out adults who impact your

child's life? Or, if you are an adult influence in a child's life, do you know of kids with no one?

Or is your school paying through grants for elderly foster grandparents? As I look around, I see more and more programs, typically grant funded, that attempt to replace family. What came first? What caused this extensive breakdown of family? What role do grant-funded government programs play in this? Let's just skip that debate and go back and evaluate the problem. Who do you think is responsible for your children? How did we get to the point of having so many young adults with children but who have no basic skills themselves? Now we have coalitions, partnerships, councils, and fill-in-the-blank — all receiving money through assorted governmental agencies.

This has done two things. It makes people reliant on government funding and programs for almost every aspect of their lives. Of greater concern to me, is now people are getting paid, minimally, to do the work that was previously done by volunteers. This is systematically destroying a major component of this American life. DeTocqueville marveled at the American marketplace — alive with associations. Now, the dominant organization is government through our schools with grants replacing the family structure.

"The more laws and orders are made prominent,
the more thieves and robbers there will be"
— Lao-tzu (604-531 BC)

"Knowledge is not simply another commodity. On the contrary. Knowledge is never used up. It increases by diffusion and grows by dispersion."
— Daniel J. Boorstein, Librarian of Congress to the House Appropriations Subcommittee, The New York Times, February 23, 1986

Chapter Twenty-one

Connect the Dots . . .

"Failure to connect the dots" was a major, constructive criticism after the tragedy of 9-11. Other problems included in the 9-11 report included communication failure. In what has become a common response in my lifetime, we created a new bureaucracy to address those problems.

I subscribe to Yogi Berra's very apt witticisms, including, "If you don't know where you've been, how will you know where you are going?"

We Boomers may not be anymore arrogant than others in the history of mankind, but I feel we're in the top ten. As you know by now, I enjoy *The Wall Street Journal*. "Don't Know Much About History" is a prime example of why. The subtitle to that article from June 18, 2011 was that popular historian David McCullough says textbooks have become "so politically correct" as to be comic." Meanwhile, Thomas Edison gets little attention.

When David McCullough calls our children "historically illiterate," it is time to pay attention.

Since this book is about education, I would like to plug his book about John Adams. It reads like a contemporary novel. The size is probably too much to expect a Generation Y person to sit and read. That is not my perspective, but one expressed on a PBS "Digital Nation" program. What I will also plug unabashedly is Bill O'Reilly's *Killing Lincoln*. Prior to TV, Bill had been a history teacher. He also writes in a concise, contemporary, but briefer style that brings life to history.

Maybe the majority of our countrymen are ready to trade free will for stability due to the current economic turmoil, but my preference would be to have our students reading the book, looking at a video or reviewing the *Cliff Notes* for *Brave New World* or *Animal Farm*. That kind of knowledge will empower them as citizens.

Whether it is national security or federal education guidelines, we do not eliminate any agencies or people, except for an occasional sacrificial lamb. We simply write new programs with the promise of a better tomorrow. Also what was once old — if you live long enough — will become new again. This is true in education and other areas in our lives. Ask any teacher with more than twenty years experience how many programs re-appear in new packaging.

As mentioned in the second chapter, I have seen geography eliminated and brought back. Now I am seeing a big focus on science again because we are falling behind in many areas, including engineering. This must be the third or fourth push on science in my lifetime.

Have you ever noticed, for example, in elementary schools, when the focus was on reading that math skills deteriorated? Then you see the focus on math and reading decline. From my observation, it seems that our schools can only maintain one focus, but that needs explanation. When the politics of the moment push for anything in education, then money follows for that emphasis – whatever it may be. Now with the current STEM programs (Science, Technology, Engineering and Math) the time, energy, money, staffing will go into those areas. What could be questionable about that? At the lower elementary level, the first focus must be on reading. All other subject areas can only build off reading. When the pendulum swings with anything, we lose a needed balanced approach.

To keep current with contemporary thinking, I recently subscribed to *The Reader's Digest*. I simply laughed out loud when I saw a bullet point: "Perk up: Your favorite morning pastime provides powerful protection against cancer and strokes - and lowers the risk of depression by 20%."

Yes, coffee! Drink more, even six cups or more can reduce men's risk of dying from prostate cancer by 60%. This was from Dr. Sanjiv Chopra, author of *Live Better, Live Longer: The New Studies That Reveal What's Really Good – and Bad – for Your Health*. He is also with the Harvard Medical School.

How does this tie into education and STEM? Has the problem again been misidentified?

If the Exxon ad is accurate showing the U.S. as 17th and 25th in the world for science and math, what is the solution? Is it a matter of rigorous standards to return? I do not think our children are less smart or able.

We have lowered our expectations for assorted reasons, most of which are lame. I think there are connections to be made. Last winter I heard a report on NPR about women not reading the warning that stipulates certain birth control measures do not prevent the spread of STDs. I'm not at all surprised by that. People can only handle so many warnings in any given period. When we built our home in 1991, I gathered all the manuals that came with all the appliances, as I thought I should look at them. Suddenly I found myself almost overwhelmed by all the warnings, particularly the add-ons for the state of California. Did you know that a gas stove may be hazardous to your health? Sometime in the 1990s major companies decided to take the most stringent state regulations to use to produce one countrywide manual. I point that out as a concrete example of the costs associated with excessive regulations. But the main reason is that there comes a point when we human beings simply tune out. How many times can we hear the cry of wolf before we ignore legitimate calls or warnings? So, as we increase regulations, are we infantilizing our society? Where does it end?

The director of "An Inconvenient Truth" also brought us "Waiting for Superman," one of the saddest videos I have seen in a while. Bill Gates in this production asks, "Where is the outrage?" How many more programs, evaluations, new-new whatever must we see before we seriously look at other alternatives? Google the names of Geoffrey

232

Canada or Michelle Rhee if you want to see viable alternatives or watch the heartache of parents seeking alternatives to public education in major cities by waiting on a lottery, hoping their child is chosen.

In October 3, 2011, the *WSJ* reported, "An African-American mother of two, Ms. Williams-Bolar, last year used her father's address to enroll her two daughters in a better public school outside of their neighborhood. After spending nine days behind bars charged with grand theft, the single mother was convicted of two felony counts. Not only did this stain her spotless record, but it threatened her ability to earn her teacher's license she had been working on."

Honestly, truth *is* stranger than fiction. Do you agree with Bill Gates? Where is our outrage?

More than ever, I think it is time to think for ourselves. Do you think you are able to connect the dots? With a voucher in hand, do you think you might find a better school for your family?

After the horrific tsunami hit Japan in April 2011, I received an e-mail making the rounds among my friends. I am sharing it because as you read it, I'd like you to consider what each response would be here in our country.

Ten Things to learn from Japan
1. THE CALM
        Not a single visual of chest-beating or wild grief. Sorrow itself has been elevated.
2. THE DIGNITY

Disciplined lines for water and groceries.
Not a rough word or a crude gesture. Their patience
is admirable and praiseworthy.
3. THE ABILITY
The incredible architects, for instance. The
buildings swayed but did not fall.
4.THE GRACE
People bought only what they needed for the
present so everybody could get something.
5. THE ORDER
No looting in shops. No honking and no
overtaking on the roads. Just understanding.
6. THE SACRIFICE
Fifty workers stayed back to pump sea water
in the N-reactors.
7. THE TENDERNESS
Restaurants cut prices. An unguarded ATM
is left alone. The strong cared for the weak.
8. THE TRAINING
The old and the children, everyone knew
exactly what to do. And they did just that.
9. THE MEDIA
They showed magnificent restraint in the
bulletins. No silly reporters. Only calm reportage.
No politicians trying to get cheap mileage.
10. THE CONSCIENCE
With the power went off in a store, people
put things back on the shelves and left quietly.

With their country in the midst of a colossal
disaster, the Japanese citizens can teach plenty of
lessons to the world.

Did your local high school, in any classes, discuss
any elements of this?

"We have inadvertently designed a system in which being good at what you do as a teacher is not formally rewarded, while being poor at what you do is seldom corrected nor penalized."
— Elliot Eisner, Stanford School of Education, The New York Times, Sept. 3, 1985

"The only thing new in the world is the history you don't know."
— Merle Miller's Plain Speaking: An Oral Biography of Harry S. Truman, 1974

Chapter Twenty-two

Always Follow the Money

Always, always follow the money!

We all really do understand that at some level and yet we constantly forget it. Why is it we are shocked when miscreants are revealed? How many very bright people and sophisticated organizations did Bernie Madoff scam? Old sayings are trite but true – annoyingly so. "If it is too good to be true, then it probably is" echoes in my head from my childhood. I had the good fortune to have two grandmothers who made references to the Great Depression by way of those types of old sayings.

What motivates most people? Nothing complicated about this: what's in it for me? WIIFM. Salespeople instinctively seem to understand this and will play to an individual's desires, wants or needs. We human beings can and are pulled into the web of make-believe, greed, gluttony, lust, anger, sloth or envy. Think about women of a certain age buying a skin product advertised by a model many, many years her junior.

Selling the opportunity to make a lot of money, Charles Ponzi in 1919 perpetuated a multi-million-dollar scam. The word "Ponzi" is part of our American lexicon, yet Madoff was able to pull one off on sophisticated investors.

The above are extreme examples of following the money but there is another component to this.

Cui bono? Who benefits? With **all** the special interests, each with lobby groups working for them, we now see winners and losers in the public and private sectors.

This isn't about just for-profit organizations. The nonprofit world wraps itself in righteousness since there are no profits, but executive salaries in that sector might surprise you. I repeat: follow the money and see who benefits.

If the various media were more industrious, there would be no need to rant for legislation about money in politics, for example. Financial reporting laws, already on the books for charities, political groups and candidates, will tell you the where/who/when of the sources of the money.

I asked a young teacher once how she felt about her union dues going to pay for political ads. She said that doesn't happen. I suggested she ask that question at the next union meeting. She was told her dues do not pay for political ads. I simply waited for the next state election, when several, full-color, expensive mailers arrived at her home. All had the notation indicating the source of funding for the ads: Massachusetts Teachers Association.

It always depends upon whose ox is to be gored but similar ads can be found from business groups, too. Even with a seventh-grade reading level, people can figure the score if the required filings were made public before an election. In my state, all candidates must file a campaign finance report eight days before an election but the information never becomes public until someone writes a book about a campaign years later. Wouldn't you like to know in a state election how much money a candidate received from out-of-state donors? Does the amount of donations matter more, or do you look at the sources? What matters to you?

It is my sincere hope that all the Internet avenues of communication will enable citizens to make more informed decisions.

Unfortunately, public union labor contract negotiations are held in executive sessions, which in my state means the meeting is not open to the public nor are any records of the meetings available until after a contract is signed. And then the minutes barely reflect what transpired, by law needing only to record any vote taken. That also includes education's public employee unions, hardly sacrosanct institutions since they are populated with human beings who also want their WIIFMs. In teachers' contract negotiations over many years I was told, "last hired, first fired" by union negotiation leaders. No matter that an extremely bright, capable, energetic young teacher might be lost with that mentality.

For a family looking at school systems, here are some questions to ask:

• What are all the terms of the contract? Not just percentage changes of money increases but also cost of additional benefits.
• How often teachers are individually evaluated?
• Do all teachers automatically receive pay increases?
• How many teachers consistently, year after year, have their students individually achieve measurable improvements?
• What part of the school budget comes from local, state, federal sources or grants from any source? I suggest this question because we no longer know the full, true cost of education. If we did, I believe we would be demanding better results for the cost.
• Have you ever asked a teacher at a parent-teacher conference what book he or she read over the summer?

In following the money, you might see inadequate staff members continuously receiving raises without performances to match. I am an avid supporter of merit pay at a minimum. In general, though, for what is spent it is time to expect more. While I am committed to an educated populace, I no longer see public education as presently constituted in this country as viable, meaningful or accomplished. I believe families making their own choices are quite capable of finding schools to meet their children's needs. With competition among schools, we can improve education. I see the Harlem School as a prime example.

How many movies do we need to see before we realize that it is the strong, dedicated teacher or principal that makes a difference? Children should not be condemned to mediocrity anywhere in this country. Always we hear laments that we do not spend enough money. I suggest that we do, but we need to see how it is allocated.

Yet I also call your attention to other areas in the public domain. How many tertiary sewage treatment systems do you see? Most municipalities do not build them because of the cost. There are several types available but not are as good as a three-stage system. Binary systems are effective, do not harm our environment and are cost effective. It seems we have lost all sense of proportion. To ask for a return on investment is not considered a part of accountability.

Last year, though, Joel Klein, former superintendent of NYC's schools, said that it is time to axe public programs that don't yield results. He described effectively in *The Wall Street Journal* (7-7-11) how both liberal and conservative subsidies linger in perpetuity. He pointed to Head Start, with a cost $ billion for one million kids a year. Do you call that fuzzy math? Head Start — not a part of the Department of Education — is the last vestige of the "War on Poverty. There are numerous reports available online that give contradicting opinions; that any positive results are gone by the end of second grade is a view held by a new and growing cohort of thinkers, including Joel Klein.

Always, always follow the money. The generation that was taught there is a free lunch seemed surprised that student loan debt topped $1 trillion in 2011. In any organization or society we need people who understand finances, for good or bad.

240

Do you as a citizen expect at minimum that a child entering seventh grade have a reading level sufficient to do the work? Do you know how many dropouts were enrolled in pre-school? Are you satisfied with the end product of our public schools for all students given what it costs?

> *"The new frontier of which I speak is not a set of promises – it is a set of challenges. It sums not what I intend to offer the American people, but what I intend to ask of them."*
> *—John Fitzgerald Kennedy,*
> *Speech accepting the Democratic Presidential nomination, July 15, 1960*

"It's really hard to design products by focus groups. A lot of times, people don't know what they want until you show it to them."
— Steve Jobs, Business Week, May 25, 1998

Chapter Twenty-three

Final Questions

As a former EMT (Emergency Medical Technician), I was taught the concept of triage. For example, in a major event such as a twenty-car pile up, it becomes necessary to do triage. This is where a very quick, 30-second or less look at each patient is made. You establish how many are dead, as that changes the total number of patients. Then you set up three categories: walking wounded, seriously injured, and mortally wounded. Care is not provided at this point and that may be the most difficult part of this process for all involved. It is only with this assessment can care be properly allocated. Is it time for triage in education?

Because of my family, I appreciate the attributes of resourcefulness and creativity. What do you value? What do you appreciate? What do you love? My late mother-in-law, in her 90-plus years of life, lived from horse and buggy rides for shopping to a man landing on the moon and then to the advent of the Internet. Our children and grands will see even more and faster changes in everything in their lifetimes. Well, almost everything. What will be the constants in your family's life? Have you thought about these types of questions? If not, then others may make decisions for you.

Are you fatigued, tired, fed-up with all the Grand Plans and Theories about everything, including education? Do you think American education has better results today than 50 years ago? Are our children better prepared to meet challenges for work? Are they as good as or better than the competition around the world?

What would you do differently if you had choices for your family's education? Is it time for vouchers, so families are able to choose better schools for their children?

At your family's school, how many teachers attended private colleges versus state colleges? Will your school find that question too invasive of teachers' privacy? Will they tell you the college class ranking of each teacher upon graduation? Will they tell you which teachers consistently show that their classes are advancing each year?

Does your family's school require any summer reading?

If you are a grandparent or a family friend, how might you help educate the current generation? Have you considered effective means of communicating with the younger ones? Do you relate contemporary events with your own life for a child to consider in a broader context?

Does your local library have e-books available to download for a certain amount of time? If not, why?

Do you think a national service requirement should be enacted for young people or do you, as a parent or guardian believing in that concept of service, believe that you are better able to direct that effort?

Have you considered giving books as gifts at a baby shower?

Is reading pertinent to your life?

Has your state at any time in the last 40 years experienced court decisions that required equitable spending across that state? What are the results of those actions? Are you satisfied with the results? Has spending more money made any significant difference? Do you feel that your child falls somewhere in the middle and is ignored?

Have you ever, by your silence or acceptance, enabled only one dominant perspective in American education? Are you going to wait for "somebody" to do "something" about American education or are you ready to take a few small steps to regain your own control of your family's education?

What will **you** do with these questions?

"Steve Jobs knew all about competitive markets. He once likened our school system to the old phone monopoly. "I remember," he said in a 1995 interview, "seeing a bumper sticker with the Bell logo on it and it said, 'We don't care. We don't have to.' And that's what a monopoly is. That's what IBM was in their day. And that's certainly what the public school system is.
They don't have to care."
—Rupert Murdoch in The Wall Street Journal, Oct. 11, 2011, on the
Steve Jobs Model for Education Reform

"It's all part of taking a chance and expanding man's horizon's. The future doesn't belong to the fainthearted, it belongs to the brave."
— President Ronald Reagan after the 1986 Challenger disaster

"The little world of childhood with its familiar surroundings is a model of the greater world. The more intensely the family has stamped its character upon the child, the more it will tend to feel and see its earlier miniature world again in the bigger world of adult life."
— *Psychological Reflections: A Jung Anthology (1953), (edited by Jolande Jacobi) p. 83: Collected Works, vol. 4, The Theory of Psychoanalysis (1913)*

Chapter 24

Jersey Shore Memories

As I was finishing this book, my very large, extended family decided to add another family gathering to our calendar since our annual December 26th Christmas party does not fit everyone's schedule. In addition to that event, another brother decided to host a Christmas-in-July party at his place in North Wildwood, NJ. Fortunately his place, also adjacent to another brother's home, backs up to an alley so we had a lot of space to set up beach chairs, baby strollers, kids' bikes, and tables loaded with food in the garages. It felt like an old-fashioned city block party.

As I sat, watched and listened, I was struck by the thought that my family is really a microcosm of the larger society. I was thinking about this because a young nephew who is an engineer, soon to be married, was engaged in a discussion of politics with his father and me a few days before the party. I was distressed at the extent of his cynicism but had to admit that our political class, epitomized by all of Congress, has broken the intergenerational and civil compacts with overall society. I understand his sense that elections no longer matter; the key difference is that members of my generation are not willing to give up their voices, whatever their viewpoints.

I do my best day dreaming, relaxing and thinking on a beach. My nephew's comments kept reverberating in my head when I realized I had deleted a section on generational differences. I thought I might have gone too far afield, yet, how could I talk about our commonality in family without looking at some of the differences? As a Boomer, I guess I always thought society would revolve around us because of our size. Silly me. In the 1980s, I attended a management seminar that touched on these vivid contrasts among generations but as I have aged I forgot about it.

The tendency in these types of reports is to analyze impacts in the workplace. But what does your local school faculty age distribution look like? Boomers have started to retire but still make up about one half of staff.

A quick look at the generations might be helpful:

Traditionalists: 1925-1942
• Duty & Honor
• Depression and WWII
(Bob Dole, George H.W. Bush, Jimmy Carter)

Baby Boomers: 1946-1964
• Self-Actualization
• Vietnam War
(Bill Clinton, Meryl Streep, and this author)

Generation X: 1964-1982
• Life Balance
• Watergate
(Barack Obama, Jennifer Lopez, my daughter)

Generation Y: 1982-2000
• Team Work
• 9/11 and corporate scandals
(Ashton Kucher, Gabby Douglas, my
grandchildren)

Perhaps the most telling difference as relates to
education is the dominant means of communication
used by each generation and compare those means
with how we educate.

Traditionalists – radio and newspapers
Baby Boomers – television
Gen X - computers
Gen Y – advanced cell phones

We will need educational managers who understand
all these differences as well as what is passed along
among generations. What does your family value?
In my first book, *The Women in the Mirror, the
Writing of a Family Memoir,* I showed the

resourcefulness and creativity among generations. What is your family's favorite depression-era resourcefulness tip that has been passed down through the generations? My kids always laughed at me for re-using pieces of aluminum foil but long before any Earth Day celebrations calling us to reduce, re-use, recycle, I was resourceful in choosing not to waste.

After the family party in North Wildwood, we headed to nearby Cape May for a week with my sister and her husband. I was pleased to see that they continue to receive a daily newspaper, *The Philadelphia Inquirer,* delivered to their door. The July 26th editorial cartoon summed up Generation Y so completely that my sister, the retired high school principal, and I completely agreed that it totally encapsulated where they are. It showed a looming, tall, dark, Batman-like figure with **"INDIFFERENCE"** emblazoned across his chest with words woven into the indifferent crusader's cape: "Kids who lack human contact or purpose * desensitized * dissolution of family * apathy * detached * vacant * insentience * hollow * dispassionate * devoid. The caption under the cartoon was "A Darkness Rising."

Many of our young people have judged us and found us wanting. Have we as a country lost our sense of stewardship for future generations? The words "lacking human contact" resonated with me. Visiting from a rural area, I admit sometimes I face culture shock when I see all the electronic devices attached to people. How long before we simply implant them at birth? Seriously, have you noticed that Generation Y does not like to talk? In chapter

18, I asked whether reading would become obsolete or an elite activity. Now I wonder if we are seeing the evolving muteness of a people. Even in the same room, young people are using devices to communicate. What happens to relationships without face-to-face contact? I have always been a letter writer so I appreciate that form of communication. But it is the almost total lack of speech that I found disconcerting. I watched many of the Gen Y family members' texting others, some within ten feet of them. I did note, though, that our family's young mothers are restricting screen usage with the little ones.

I saw an ad for Verizon's FIOS that said, "everything has to be faster now" and that probably explains a lot too. However, choices can be made. On our vacation with the TV off, we sat at the kitchen table playing board games with our grandchildren. That involved a lot of spontaneous laughter and giggles while creating sweet memories for them.

My family, until this time, has seen each generation receive more education, pursue home ownership, and work to help the upcoming generation. I grew up believing and knowing that a citizen could fight City Hall and win.

When we bought our first home in Massachusetts for $19,500 in 1970, we were shocked at our first tax bill that had an assessment value of $22,000. While the amount may appear small now, trust me, it was a scary amount to our household budget. I went to Town Hall, spoke with staff in the assessors' office, got the real run around and was at my wits' end. My husband told me there was nothing we could do about it because you can't fight City Hall. I contacted the builder, who suggested I drive around town, find similar properties, and go back to Town Hall to see how they were assessed. There was a huge ledger on the counter serving the public so you could look up assessments for every address. I spent hours, but I developed a list of properties the same size — some even bigger — obtained the assessed values and found that all of them were assessed $12,000-$15,000.

I later learned that some local people considered it a game to give newcomers a difficult time and, when possible, that included higher assessments. It is that most unflattering human trait of seeing "the other" as fair game. Eventually this practice ended with state law requiring assessments every three years to maintain an approximate 100% of valuation. But, to make a long story short, I was able to get a corrected assessment at $14,500 because I fought Town Hall.

I find in many ways I understand my nephew's cynicism but I am not ready to cede the battle, hence this book. I am discouraged that many people blame all the money in politics. Here in my town this year we had a non-binding resolution at our annual town meeting calling for a Constitutional amendment prohibiting corporations (no others) from contributing in anyway to a political campaign. I prepared a statement against the petition. In a few minutes, I was able to get information from a government site for campaign donations in 2010 and early results for 2012. The

Federal Elections Commission report is available to anyone. In a nutshell, I found each party and its affiliates received similar amounts. Yes, they are huge amounts but I place more confidence in the American voter to figure out who's buying and who's selling. It would help if the media chose to report these filings. Perhaps most distressful was a comment made on town meeting floor: "while you (Marguerite) are able to find this information, most people can't and they need to be protected by the government." I guess this is confirmation that our children's reading levels are less than fifth grade and many think our government can create a risk-free world. This is a concrete example where schools have failed to produce citizens who can read and think for themselves. How sad.

I concluded my remarks with " . . .knowledge is power and we should not regulate any person's speech. This motion speaks to our democracy. Just because it is said does not make it true. We are not a democracy. We are a democratic republic that needs active citizenship, not more legislation attempting to regulate behavior." Citizenship requires education.

My family has unity in some areas, great disparities in others, but our concept of family is our underlying strength. My sister Rosemarie and I had the great pleasure of watching our grandchildren playing on the beach, using their boogey boards, building sand castles and carefully eating sandwiches under big beach umbrellas so the seagulls could not swoop in and steal their food. Here at the Jersey Shore those of my generation get to teach a new generation what family means. Over a Scrabble board we encourage competition. With the game of Boggle we are able to let the younger ones enter the game with two-letter words while increasing the requirements as they get older.

At the family party, my son was telling me about a pond in Plymouth, MA where he and his wife like to canoe. One Sunday the park was filled with Brazilian-Americans. He said while he did not understand their language, he did enjoy their music. Of note, though, was the presence of several generations from infants to very old folks. He said it was a large, extended family simply having fun at a public park. The group's interaction reminded him of our family. In my youth we were day-trippers going to the Jersey Shore with the station wagon packed with food, bathing suits, towels, buckets and shovels. How does your family get together? What memories, standards, skills and life guidelines are you creating for your children or grandchildren?

We are seeing exponential changes in many areas, including education. I saw advertisements for cyber charter schools in Pennsylvania and New Jersey. The first, Agora Cyber Charter Schools, are tuition-free public schools online. This is something to watch, as others will also develop. My first reaction was "finally, a viable alternative for a teenager who sees school as an imprisonment." Additionally, cyber schools increase our possible choices and can also reduce the cost of education. We haven't even begun to see what all our options may be in the future.

With all the changes coming, what choices will your family make? What choices do you want to give up?

> *"An unconditional right to say what one pleases about public affairs is what I consider to be the minimum guarantee of the First Amendment"*
> *— S.C. Justice Hugo Black, NY Times Company v. Sullivan, 376 U.S., 254 (1964)*

"Teaching is an instinctual art, mindful of potential, craving of realizations, a pausing, seamless process"
– A. Bartlett Giamatti, Yale President, in "The American Teacher,"
Harpers, July 1980

Acknowledgements

The very first notes I scribbled for this book started as an actual physical file with a scrap of paper on which I wrote, "Read to me, Mom-mom." I knew deep within myself that another book was taking shape even while I was working on my first book, "The Women in the Mirror – the Writing of a Family Memoir." I have come to see how being a grandmother has so shaped this time in my life. I am so grateful for this experience and trust that my grandchildren will not be offended, embarrassed or annoyed that I write about them.

I have been blessed in my life to know many fine teachers, many in my own family. I am grateful to them all.

My parents, Rosemarie and James J. Taylor, my first teachers;
My daughter, Marguerite Rancourt, who has always inspired me with her creative and resourceful efforts;
My sister, Rosemarie Farrow, for her gentle temperament but strong beliefs;
My sister, Kate Taylor, who epitomizes life-long learning;

My godson, Brian McGill, a great English literature teacher;

My niece, Rachel Farrow, an imaginative elementary school teacher;

My nephew, Kevin Farrow and his wife Melissa, outstanding math teachers who could easily and profitably pursue other endeavors;

My nephew, David John Taylor, Jr., who gave me the idea for the last chapter;

Gail Roberts, for sharing the pattern of the teacher reading to her students;

My late, life-long friend, Dr. Francine Perrine-Wittkamp, who encouraged me to write;

The late Sister Mary Eleanor, GNSH and her inspiring words to me;

Joseph Sciaccia, formerly of Commercial Union Insurance Company, who taught me so much about teaching;

Jeanne Bruffee, who trusted me in her classroom;

Becky Schaefer, who saw my granddaughter's potential;

Nancy Henderson, who helped my granddaughter fulfill that potential;

Sylvia Davenport, gas station owner/operator, for uncommon candor;

Frank Carcio, funny friend and a lawyer who admits to not knowing everything;

Maryanne Chorba, for her Boxerish dedication and amazing skills;

Jack Maurer, for fifty-plus years, still loving the kids.

Made in the USA
Lexington, KY
17 October 2013